LEGAL PAGE

Women!

Book 2: The Spirit of the Fox
© Shan 2023

Published by Clear Mind Press
2023 Alice Springs Australia

ISBN Print book: 978-0-6457074-8-9

ISBN eBook: 978-0-6457074-9-6

Cover design by Clear Mind Press
Photo cover: Image by Pexels

All rights reserved. Except as permitted under the Australian Copyright Act 1968 (for example, fair dealing for study, research, criticism or review), no part of this book may be reproduced, stored in a retrieval system, communicated or transmitted in any form or by any means without prior written permission.

All inquiries should be made to the publisher.

info@clearmindpress.com
https://www.clearmindpress.com

Women!

Women!

Book 2: The Spirit of the Fox

Shan

Clear Mind Press

CONTENTS

	LEGAL PAGE	i
1	Ground Zero: Alice Springs 2023	1
2	The visit of the Spirit of the Fox	3
3	Place one: The incubator	16
4	Place two: The Jewish quarter of Amsterdam	24
5	Place three: Etersheim, the Netherlands	32
6	Place four: Hoorn, the Netherlands	38
7	Place five: Gorinchem, the Netherlands	44
8	Place six: Arkel, the Netherlands	49
9	Place seven: Pont Aven, Bretagne, France	54
10	Place eight: Amersfoort, the Netherlands	59
11	Place nine: De Pinte, Belgium	67

CONTENTS

12 | Place ten: Leiden, the Netherlands 77

13 | Place eleven: Evergem, Belgium 82

14 | Place twelve: Ghent, Belgium 90

15 | The Turning Point 98

16 | The diagnosis 104

17 | The aftermath 113

18 | Rik Schipper, at last 137

19 | Huis ten Bosch, Nagasaki 145

ABOUT THE BOOK 155
ABOUT THE AUTHOR 157

1

Ground Zero: Alice Springs 2023

I had made a large pot of soup from scratch. I started it two days earlier by soaking and boiling the chickpeas. This caused a massive mess on the stove, but it made a lovely base once ground to a smooth paste with miso and cashew butter.

When the soup was finished with parsley, kidney beans, and capsicum and ready to eat, I divided it into two pots and took one to Marilyn.

The dog stood in the door frame.

"Gus, what do you want?" I said, "Go inside or outside?"

"Let him in if he wants to," Marilyn called from above.

The dog and I climbed the stairs to Marilyn's kitchen.

Marilyn made tea and served date cake with thick salted butter.

"Here, fresh from the oven, it's still warm."

We drank our tea and ate our cake in comfortable silence while looking at the tops of the trees, which slightly wave in the wind, causing a kaleidoscopic light effect on the walls. "I cannot even see your cottage anymore said Marilyn. "These trees are growing like mad."

"Aren't they now," I agreed.

"Let's sit on the balcony."

We took our tea and cake outside.

"Another crystal-clear day in paradise."

"Yes."

Gus lay between us in a sunny spot and looked from one to another while we were talking.

"Nice date cake, not too sweet."

"Fresh from the date farm. These camels were lounging across the road when I drove back to town. They did not want to move."

"Did you get out of the car?"

"No, there was a bull amongst them that looked like you'd better not cross him, hey Gus."

"Good dog."

I patted the dog.

We sat in silence.

I returned to my stove and placed the other pot of soup in the fridge for later.

A couple of hours later, when I opened the refrigerator, the pot jumped out as if it were alive, spilling nearly all its contents on the floor and against the wall. It was as if someone had projectile-vomited, aiming to cause as much damage as possible.

I mopped up the goo while swearing.

That evening, I placed the remainder of the soup in the pot on the stove to warm, and I walked away from it for a second. When I returned, the lid was covered in ants. Despite a ton of anti-ant powder everywhere, they had already made it into the soup. The Outback and its bloody ants!

After all that work, I had no soup left at all. I found this typical of the world of women, the Willing Slaves of the West.

It also somehow reminded me of my family of origin.

2

The visit of the Spirit of the Fox

I met Kunikaze in Tokyo while working as a hostess at the nightclub Pussy Cat. He was a likable fellow compared to most businessmen who frequented the club. He looked like an average Japanese young man when he wasn't wearing his hopelessly old-fashioned Burberry suit. He held the position of *kacho* in a large advertising firm and believed that advertising was information. I thought this was naive. His English was not excellent, but it was better than that of most Japanese. He was an avid reader and had a sizable library, mainly consisting of European books in Japanese. Like many Japanese men, he enjoyed having alcohol in the evenings and dining out. Our interest in dining out was the only thing we had in common. Sharing an apartment had several advantages. For him, it meant 'more prestige' if we pretended to be partners. Every *kacho* was expected to have a wife, and having a foreign wife was even better, instantly making him popular among his co-workers. For me, it meant a visa and no longer being pursued by Japanese men. The difference was immediate and a relief. For both of us, it meant shared rent and some company. Kunikaze liked to watch TV at home, so he was low maintenance.

We found a beautiful two-bedroom apartment in Musashi Koganei overlooking the leafy campus of *Keizai Daigaku*, the University for Economics. We furnished it tastefully. Before we knew it, we had settled into a somewhat monotonous routine, which I tried to counterbalance by taking up painting and writing again. I painted small oil paintings on wooden panels depicting street scenes and shopfronts. I wrote short stories about daily life in Japan. Continuing to work at the nightclub was no longer an option due to its negative impact on Kunikaze's professional reputation. Instead, we often had my friends over in the evenings or went out on the town. I had a couple of English teaching jobs and worked fewer hours than ever before. This might have contributed to the bewildering events that followed.

Shortly after settling into the apartment, I attended a Dutch film festival to watch the movie *De smaak van water* (The Taste of Water) at a movie theatre in Yoyogi. The screening was scheduled for eleven in the morning. I went alone. Reaching the theatre took forty-five minutes on a train and a short walk. The morning rush had subsided, and hardly any people were on the train. I felt strangely unsettled, though I couldn't pinpoint why. I navigated my way from Yoyogi Station to the theatre using a map. In Tokyo, where street names are non-existent, directions are often given using old-fashioned, hand-drawn maps. It involved instructions like: "Turn left at the big tree" or "Turn right at the laundry...."

Only a few people were in the ultra-modern cinema complex, and the theatre where the movie was playing was empty.

It felt strange to hear the Dutch language and see familiar images of the Jewish Quarter in Amsterdam on the screen while being so far away from it.

The black-and-white film revolves around Hes, a disillusioned social worker nearing retirement, who discovers a young woman named Anna in the closet in the house of a deceased acquaintance. Realising that she has been confined to the apartment her entire life, he decides to help her navigate the complexities of the real world. The girl lives in an old canal house reminiscent of the one I grew up in. Her appearance is more animal-like than human. Despite that, Hes manages to forge a connection with her.

As I watched the story unfold, something strange happened. First, I lost track of the storyline. A spell seemed to be taking hold of me. I blinked a few times and shook my head, but the condition persisted.

Then, the theatre walls seemed to cave in, and my vision became incredibly sharp, making everything appear distant as if viewed through the wrong end of a pair of binoculars. Sounds became faint and echoed as if I were hearing them through a tunnel.

Alarmed, I attempted to stand up but stumbled back into my seat as the floor seemed to shake violently. Thoughts of an earthquake raced through my mind: The dreaded "big one." Tokyo experienced minor tremors a few times a week and occasionally stronger ones, but upon closer examination, this situation seemed unrelated to the environment. Instead, my perception of reality was disintegrating, crumbling like dry sand, sometimes forming cubes, sometimes bubbles, not unlike when on LSD. Once I realised this, I mustered the courage to try and leave the cinema, breathing heavily.

Outside were only a few people. They appeared distant and indistinct. Moving became incredibly difficult. It felt as if I were walking on water in a two-dimensional world. After walking a distance away from the theatre, I became violently ill and vomited into a nearby garbage bin. It was not unlike having sea sickness. Hoping that the vomiting would have alleviated my symptoms, I looked around anxiously. Had I consumed something poisonous? Did anyone witness me getting sick? I tried to recall what I had eaten in the past twenty-four hours, but my thoughts were muddled. It was impossible to think clearly. The square where I stood seemed to stretch out indefinitely in every direction, its shape warping at the horizon. Distorted traffic sounds reached my ears. Did someone drug me? Was anyone aware of my condition? Was there anyone here at all? I now couldn't see any people, only the empty square.

As I began crossing the vast square, heading in what I hoped was the station's direction, I felt as if I were hanging by a thread. I knew with absolute certainty that if that thread were to snap, I would be dead. It was that thread that supplied me with an energy akin to electricity. Without it, I would collapse, much like the cinema's walls. I teetered on the edge of such an event, navigating the unstable ground as best I could. It reminded me of a childhood fair attraction called the shake-a-walk. I worried that my gait appeared odd and that people would think I was insane. I stumbled through the streets for an eternity, overwhelmed by fear and shame.

Somehow, I managed to find the train station and board a train. I took the Odakyu line to Shinjuku and successfully transferred to the Chuo line. I could do so only because I had made this journey countless times before. Navigating through the crowds in my current state was a terrifying experience. On the Chuo line, a memory of another fair attraction from my childhood resurfaced: the caterpillar ride, known as *de rups*. The train seemed to bounce up and down. I had to tightly grip the armrest to avoid being thrown from my seat. Multiple dissonant melodies played simultaneously, reminiscent of a symphony by Charles Ives. My knuckles turned white from the intensity of my grip.

Once I had reached Musashi Koganei Station, I flagged down a taxi. The driver bombarded me with questions:

"Where are you from?

How do you like Japan?

How come you speak Japanese?

Can you eat with chopsticks?...."

I answered that I was unwell and asked him to leave me alone. I rested my arms on the seat before me and placed my head on my arms as if preparing for a turbulent aeroplane ride. I heard the taxi driver ask:

"*Daijobu desuka*? Are you okay?"

When finally in front of our apartment building, I handed him a ten-thousand-yen bill, and he carefully counted the change into my trembling palm. His sharp gaze intensified my fear, causing another wave of anxiety to wash over me.

Kunikaze was at work. I was alone at home. The apartment was eerily silent. The weather was unusually clear. I could see Mount Fuji from the window. I spread a futon on the tatami room floor and curled up in the foetal position. This only seemed to worsen the situation, as fragmented shards of glass now appeared to rain down from the ceiling. I broke into a sweat despite feeling cold. Dislodged thoughts raced through my mind. I desperately tried to recall what I had eaten. I rolled onto my back, extended my arms, and whispered, "Okay, okay, take me if you must. I don't care if I die."

In that moment of surrender, the overwhelming fear ceased somewhat. I must have drifted off to sleep.

Upon awakening, I realised that the situation had not improved one bit. I was paralysed with terror. A dull, metallic pain had settled in the back of my head and neck, just above my spine.

In the evening, Kunikaze helped me breathe into a paper bag, hoping to alleviate my distress.

"I need to go to the hospital," I pleaded, convinced that something was seriously wrong with my brain.

Kunikaze contacted his sister-in-law, Yukie, who promptly came over and began helping. She cleaned, cooked, and never took a moment to rest.

"Yukie," I pleaded, "I need a hospital, not food. And we have a cleaner, so please stop." But Yukie continued sweeping, washing, rinsing, baking, and frying because that was all she knew. It felt like we had an unrelenting robot in the house, and I couldn't turn it off. The smell of food made me sick again, and I vomited in the toilet. It took a day or two for Kunikaze and Yukie to comprehend that I needed medical attention.

Kunikaze took a day off work and called a taxi. Both he and Yukie had spent considerable time searching for a suitable doctor. Kunikaze appeared more fearful of me than concerned about the symptoms I was experiencing, while Yukie wanted me to eat.

"I don't want to eat!" I cried. "Can't you tell I am sick?"

She stared at me and brushed away a tear.

Kunikaze remained silent in the taxi, which I found insensitive of him. He could at least reassure me. I was sick in *his* country; he should take the lead.

"There's something wrong with my brain," I said to the doctor, pointing to the area of pain in the back of my head. I described my symptoms. Kunikaze and the doctor exchanged glances. Were they judging the *gaijin*? Were they taking me seriously? I breathed heavily throughout the consultation, and finally, the doctor agreed to perform an MRI scan. Before we left the consultation room to wait for the results, the doctor sold Kunikaze Amway products: vitamins and other powders and pills. Kunikaze paid the hefty bill in cash, having foreseen the Amway costs. He had kept the money in the breast pocket of his suit. He never carried this much cash. This did not inspire trust in me, nor did the fact that the doctor smoked a thick cigar during the consultation.

The MRI revealed no abnormalities in my brain. We returned home with bags of Amway products, realising we had spent more than a month's salary. In the taxi, I argued with Kunikaze about it. He appeared just as powerless as I felt, and I resented him. I believe he should take charge and show leadership. I despised how he had aligned himself with the doctor and wasted money on the senseless Amway products.

The symptoms worsened in the subsequent days. I experienced nearly constant hallucinations. The closest comparison I could make was to the effects of LSD. I knew what it was like to be on LSD, but I hesitated to mention this to the doctor, unsure if it would result in being confined. I didn't dare bring it up with Kunikaze, as drugs were strictly taboo in Japan. It started to occur to me that it would be best to steer clear of the Japanese medical system altogether. The idea of someone poisoning my food with LSD crossed my mind again.

After a few days, I underwent another scan at the same hospital. The entire nightmarish sequence repeated itself. The white coat. The thick cigar. Another hundred thousand yen worth of Amway products. The scan once again showed no abnormalities in my head. I was then subjected to a thorough physical examination, during which all my bodily functions were assessed. This was called *human dock*. On a physical level, there was no apparent issue. This only intensified my fear.

After selling Kunikaze a third load of Amway products, the doctor suggested seeing a psychiatrist. The total bill now amounted to 560,000 yen.

Me? Seeing a psychiatrist? What for? Just the word itself, *seshinkai*. Did they think I was insane? Did I? Was I?

In the taxi home, I told Kunikaze to cease all further contact with the Japanese medical system. I was terrified to be locked up somewhere. Hence, Kunikaze went back to work, and Yukie went back home.

Once alone, I called my American friend, Arturo, and explained to him what was happening. I was in tears. Arturo came over straight away.

"What are they? Why do I have them?" I asked, referring to the anxiety attacks.

"You need to find an American therapist to help you with these. There is only one in Tokyo that I know of - Dr Vossberg," Arturo suggested.

He made some phone calls and got me an appointment in two weeks.

He sat with me and tried to provide comfort.

"Shush now, shhh. It is all unfolding, moment by moment. Shhh," he said.

His words perplexed me. What did he know that I didn't? *It is all unfolding, moment by moment.* These words filled me with terror. I felt overwhelmed by everything, by every word spoken. The pain in my head intensified. It spread to my lower back. My brain was on fire, and I frequently held my head in both hands.

Two weeks passed, each day marked by these extraordinary circumstances. I lived in constant fear for my life, but then again, wasn't I already in hell? Wasn't I already dead? The burning ache in my back felt like a scorching pot lodged inside my skull, with a searing rod extending down to my hips.

I described all these bewildering symptoms to Doctor Vossberg during my long-awaited consultation. He was an elderly man who listened attentively and offered few words. He carefully examined the MRI scan on an old lightbox.

"What's wrong with me?"

"I don't know," he replied calmly, "but we'll find out."

We, he said. He had used the word *we*. I didn't feel so alone anymore. A glimmer of hope blinked at me.

"You need to understand first that I cannot prescribe any medication. I am not licensed to prescribe in Japan. We must tackle this without relying on chemicals. Day by day. Week by week." His confidence in this approach was evident.

"But what is the matter with me?"

"The mind is a powerful entity," he replied. "Let's talk."

"Talk about what? I've already shared everything: the headaches, the hallucinations. It feels like a chemical issue, like LSD."

"You might be onto something there."

"Do you think someone, or something, is poisoning me?"

"No, it's not that. The brain produces various substances and sends them around the body. "Let's talk."

"I don't know what to say. What is there to talk about?"

He spoke with infinite compassion: "Imagine being on the ground, broken and in pain. Wouldn't you want your mother to pick you up and hold you in her arms?"

I stared at him, tears streaming down my cheeks. "A crying mother."

"Let's start there," he said. "A crying mother. What does that mean to you?"

Words escaped my throat without my control. They flowed like molten lava, forming thick streams that cascaded downward and solidified. I listened to my voice, and the words were as new to me as they were to Dr Vossberg.

"My father...." I began." My father has grown within me like a relentless weed. He has taken control of my mind now that I'm in a country he knows nothing about. He has invaded me like a plant with roots that flow through my blood and infest my limbs. I don't know who I am. I have always lived in the shadow of his presence, and now that shadow has consumed me. He sits on my shoulder when I'm awake and whispers in my ear. He sits on the other shoulder when I sleep and whispers in the opposite ear. I want to uproot him from within me like a poisonous weed." I gestured with my hands as if pulling weeds from the top of my head. "Even the words I speak are his words. I need to find my identity, not his, or I'll wither away or die."

"You are probably right," Dr Vossberg said.

I stared at him in disbelief. Had he just acknowledged that I might not be crazy? "You mean...you don't think I'm insane?"

"You are the master of your mind. You possess the deepest understanding of your experiences."

I pondered his words. How could it be any other way? I began recounting moments of my life to him, such as my mother's constant tears and the night when I had lain beside my father at the age of twelve, as I had done when I was younger, and how he had tried to embrace me like a man embraces a woman who is not his daughter. I confessed that I blamed myself for that moment. I had become a young woman and momentarily forgotten the boundaries. The floodgates of my memories opened. I spoke of the poison coursing through my veins and the overwhelming guilt I felt after that incident. As I continued speaking, I noticed that my hands went numb. I informed Vossberg of this, but he encouraged me to continue. "Pay no mind to your hands. They will regain sensation when they decide to do so."

"So, this isn't dangerous?"

"As long as you don't attempt to harm yourself, the numbness is not dangerous. It can be frightening and inconvenient, but it will eventually pass."

"How can you be so sure?"

"Everything in life passes, does it not?"

I contemplated his words for a moment. "Except death," I said.

"Except death," he agreed.

He allowed me to unleash the torrent of words. I spoke about the innocent love I had shared with Fransje, the child-man, and how the poison had coursed through my veins whenever anyone else touched me after the incident with my father.

Vossberg interrupted my narrative. "Sexual abuse by a caregiver has a profound and long-lasting impact. The experience causes significant psychological trauma, leading to guilt, shame, and fear. Children who have been sexually abused often develop mental health problems such as depression, anxiety, and post-traumatic stress disorder. They struggle with forming and maintaining healthy relationships due to trust issues and other emotional difficulties. They frequently encounter sexual problems later in life, such as difficulties with intimacy, sexual dysfunction, and a distorted perception of sexual relationships."

His words took me by surprise. "Was I sexually abused?"

"Well, based on what you've just shared, it does align with the effects of sexual abuse."

"Does that mean I was sexually abused?"

"What do *you* think? Can you see yourself in the description I provided?"

"Yes, I can. And at the same time, it feels like I'm betraying my father by sharing all of this."

"We will need to meet three times a week," Vossberg suggested. "You've already spoken for three and a half hours today. It's time to pause."

"What about my hands? Not only do I suffer from headaches, hallucinations, and a searing pain in my back, but now my hands are numb, too." I stared at my hands. "These hands belong to my father."

"There is nothing we can do to change that now," Vossberg said. "You must bear it. My role is to accompany you on this journey through your pain. Remember what we said earlier? 'Everything passes.'".

"Everything passes. This too shall pass."
"This too shall pass."
Did I truly believe it?
"The snake poison was your saviour," said Vossberg.
I looked at him in surprise.
"It protected you from the situation to go any further."
"Hm, I've never seen it that way," I said. "But you are right."

In the following months, my visits to Vossberg were my only lifeline. They were the only respite amid the pitch-black sea I was traversing during a blizzard. A tempest raged within me, and all I could do was endure. Any attempts to distract me were met with punishing onslaughts of glassy rain, icy thunder, impenetrable mist, towering waves, numb hands, and distorted senses. I paid no attention to Kunikaze, who must have been equally terrified. The world fluctuated between flatness and multidimensionality, oscillating between black and white and vibrant. I saw non-existent colours. It was an endless rollercoaster ride, a free fall without a bottom in sight, a spinning barrel with no stop button. Every day, I heard my mother's voice calling my name, just my name, "Shan!" It was a call I knew I had to bear, to unravel and lay bare before Vossberg. I spared no detail. The scorching debris erupted ceaselessly from within me, propelled by an invisible force. It filled the shabby room with its dirty carpet, which served as Vossberg's consultation room in the old Baptist church in Shibuya.

Vossberg remained unafraid and steadfast in the face of my madness, my desperation. I wailed and howled, likening my situation to the *kitsune*, the Spirit of the Fox, from an ancient Zen tale.

"Naming it isn't a bad idea," Vossberg commented. "Let's call it *kitsune*."

Alice Springs 2023

Marilyn and I were driving to Desert Park. Marilyn had convinced me to leave my cave and "enjoy some sunshine".

"The *kitsune*, often depicted in Japanese folklore, was believed to be an intelligent creature capable of taking on human form," I shared with her in the car. "They were associated with Inari, a Shinto spirit known for its supernatural abilities. The *kitsune's* power increased with the number of tails it possessed, sometimes up to nine. Foxes were also seen as witch-like beings, untrustworthy goblins."

"That's really interesting," said Marilyn.

"The kitsune propelled me forward, guiding me through the relentless snowstorm I was experiencing. In the darkness, Doctor Vossberg was my guiding light. I revealed every detail to him, recounting everything documented in the memoir. He responded with few words. I made a list of the places I had lived and visited, shaping my narrative around these locations. I told Vossberg that places resemble lovers—they leave their imprints on us."

"That's deep," said Marilyn.

"Vossberg embraced this approach of a narrative tied to specific places."

"He sounds like a great doctor," Marilyn said.

"He was. He was already old then. He must be long dead."

Google him," said Marilyn.

I took my phone from my bag.

"He was married to a Japanese woman: Etsuko Sato Vossberg, age 76, widow of Dr. Robert Vossberg, died May 10, 2010. A celebration of her life will be at 2 p.m. Thursday, May 27, at St. Boniface Church, 5615 Midnight Pass Road, Sarasota, officiated by Pastor Ted Copeland. The Sato family in Japan will hold a Japanese service.

She was born in Akita Prefecture in northern Japan to a Christian minister father and a schoolteacher mother. An accomplished violinist and pianist, she earned a degree in American and English Literature and a master's degree in psychology, both from Rikkyo University in Japan. She came to the U.S.A. on a Fullbright scholarship to study at Columbia University. Later she attained a position at Dartmouth University, where she met her husband, Dr. "Bob" Vossberg. Her focus was on communication within the family unit, and his was on the teaching and practice of psychiatry at Dartmouth.

Eventually, they returned to Japan, he as a psychiatric doctor, lieutenant commander U.S. Navy, and she as a professor at Rikkyo University in Tokyo. Etsuko authored several books and numerous articles in psychiatry journals. She is much admired by her former students and was in the mainstream of bringing empowerment to Japanese women.

During retirement back in the U.S.A., Etsuko was active in the St. Boniface Church on Siesta Key and sang in the choir. A friend reminisced that during a tea ceremony, Etsuko serenaded the sinking sun, a memorable happening. Her friends and family remember her with affection for her ability to listen and give perceptive counsel.

Published by Herald Tribune from May 23 to May 24, 2010."

"So, he died before her."

"Yes. Rest in Peace, dear Doctor Vossberg. I owe my life to you."

3

Place one: The incubator

"Have you thought about how you want to structure these consultations?" asked Vossberg.

"I would like to move from place to place like we did in my childhood."

"That's a good idea. Name your place."

"Place One: the incubator: My first home—a glass box in a hospital in Hoorn, the Netherlands. It was a place where I emerged from the clutches of death. I seem to remember loneliness and despair," I said.

"It is doubtful that you recall your time in an incubator, but please continue."

"I beg to differ; I think I remember voices and hearing my bloodstream; there were shimmering light and round shapes above me."

"Those are probably imagined."

"From the family narrative, I know I weighed a kilogram, like a bag of sugar, and was fragile. No one was permitted to touch me for several months. I became one of those famed rhesus monkeys who grow up clinging to a barbed wire mother."

"Ah, you know about that experiment."

"Yes. I researched incubator children at the English library downstairs. It is not encouraging. Children born prematurely in the 1950s and placed in incubators were at a high risk of respiratory distress syndrome, which impeded their breathing and often necessitated mechanical ventilation. Premature birth and prolonged hospitalisation heightened the likelihood of neurodevelopmental issues, including developmental delays, learning difficulties, and behavioural problems. Poor weight gain was a prevalent concern as incubators primarily focused on maintaining warmth rather than fostering optimal growth and development. The lack of effective infection control practices increased the risk of infections."

"My word! You're a walking encyclopedia!"

"I am obsessed with premature babies."

"You are trying to understand yourself. I am a doctor of the mind," replied Vossberg. "I know that the psychological effects of being born premature and spending four months in an incubator in the 1950s may indeed include developmental delays that impact cognitive, emotional, and social development; attachment difficulties due to prolonged hospitalisation and separation from the mother; learning difficulties such as memory, attention, and problem-solving challenges; and behavioural problems such as hyperactivity, impulsivity, and aggression."

"Great! What a glamorous beginning! I have experienced most of these conditions, except perhaps aggression."

"Look at it from a different perspective: You are not solely a victim but a survivor too. Despite the challenges, you demonstrated tremendous resilience."

I was moved by his compassion and taken aback by his reframing. It felt good to be called a survivor and resilient.

"Thank you!" But how can I rid myself of the father within? How can I remove him from my mind, heart, and blood? I resemble him. Every time I look in the mirror, I see him."

"There is one huge saving grace."

"What is it? Please tell me."

"Can't you see it? It's obvious!"

"I'm afraid I don't. What is it?"

"You are a female!"

"And?"

"Your dad is a male!"

"And?"

"The female brain and behaviour differ significantly from their male counterparts. I suggest embracing your femininity. For example, your appearance now leans more towards a boyish look. Perhaps you could consider making some changes?"

"Okay. That's a good idea. I will let my hair grow and start wearing dresses again, just like when I used to do ballet."

"Think like a woman."

"I should invite Mum to Japan and spend time with her, connect through our shared femininity."

"Wait a little until you're feeling better."

"Fair enough,"

A glimmer of hope! It didn't mean that my symptoms had disappeared. They hadn't. But I took an initial step towards recovery: I purchased some dresses and stopped getting my hair trimmed. Kunikaze liked it. This, unreasonably, irritated me. I was increasingly getting irritated by Kunikaze. It wasn't fair, but I couldn't stop it. The irritation only went away when I drank wine. When we drank together, the tensions diminished, and the differences melted away.

China Moon

"I would like to invite my mother to Japan," I said.

Kunikaze and I were having dinner at China Moon in Kokubunji. Their *shumai* dumplings were terrific.

"Wait a bit, Shan, until you're feeling better."

"That's exactly what Vossberg said."

"Good!"

I thought about our beautiful apartment and our uneventful but fortunate life. I could find no gratitude for it in me. What would Dad think of it? There it was! What would Dad think of it? This was my illness! The what-would-Dad-think-of-it disease. Why did I want to know what Dad thought of my life with Kunikaze? What would I do with his rejection or approval? Why did I need his approval? Why did I *want* it? It was useless to ask these questions to Kunikaze, who was practical only. I had to come to terms with these questions on my own. I made a mental note to take them to Vossberg.

Kunikaze filled our glasses with dark brown Chinese wine. "*Kanpai*."

"*Kanpai*."

"When you're better, you can invite your father too."

"He doesn't want to come to Japan."

"Why not?"

"Because of the war."

"Which war?"

"World War II."

"But that's forty years ago."

"He won't change his mind."

"Maybe we can go to Europe and visit him then."

"Yes, let's, but don't expect it to be pleasant."

I thought of Kunikaze meeting my children. What would *they* think? That was a much better question.

"Let's start with getting Mum to Japan. I've got some apologies to make to her."

"About what?"

"Never mind. Things from the past."

"Ah."

I never told Kunikaze about my past. He knew I was divorced and had two children; that was about it. Was that healthy? Yes, it was. No, it wasn't. Why was I so confused all the time? I quickly drank the Chinese wine.

"Is everything to your liking?" the waitress wanted to know in Japanese. She had directed the question to Kunikaze, ignoring me.

We embarked on a regular game we played:

"I don't speak Japanese," said Kunikaze to her in English, "you'd better ask her." He gestured at me.

The waitress looked at me in disbelief.

"The food is delicious, the wine even better, thank you," I said in rapid Japanese.

The waitress looked from me to Kunikaze and back with mounting confusion.

"You heard what she said," said Kunikaze in English.

"Is anything wrong?" I asked in Japanese.

A perfectly round tear appeared in the left eye of the waitress, jumped over her eyelid and ran down her cheek. She covered her mouth with one hand and ran off.

"Ah, poor girl," I said, "let's explain it to her."

"No," said Kunikaze, "people should learn that not all Japanese-looking people speak Japanese and that some foreigners speak Japanese."

"But that tear! Poor thing."

"She'll get over it."

"Oh dear," I laughed.

"You laughed."

"And?"

"I haven't seen you laugh in months."

I massaged my cheeks. Kunikaze was right.

"You are getting better."

"Oh, I do hope so, Kunikaze!"

"Of course you are, Shan."

"It depends on what I have. We don't have a diagnosis yet."

"I'm sure you'll be alright."

"Based on what?" I snapped. I could not help it. I did not even feel sorry for being a sour puss. What the heck was wrong with me? I felt numb, like a serial killer.

Cozy Corner

Kunikaze, always the practical one, insisted that I should leave the house at least once every day. He asked me to meet him for lunch at Cozy Corner and teach him some English.

"Do you want coffee?" he asked.

"I can't have caffeine, I'm afraid. I'll have an iced green tea."

Kunikaze ordered.

"What do you want me to teach you?"

"Read me a page of English."

I opened the book I was reading on a random page.

"The so-called black sheep of the family are, in fact, hunters born of paths of liberation into the family tree.

The members of a tree who do not conform to the norms or traditions of the family system, those who since childhood have constantly sought to revolutionise beliefs, going against the paths marked by family traditions, those criticised, judged and even rejected, these are usually called to free the tree of repetitive stories that frustrate entire generations.

The black sheep, those who do not adapt, those who cry rebelliously, play a basic role within each family system; they repair, pick up and create new and unfold branches in the family tree.

Thanks to these members, our trees renew their roots. Its rebellion is fertile soil; its madness is water that nourishes; its stubbornness is new air; its passion is fire that re-ignites the light of the heart of the ancestors.

Uncountable repressed desires, unfulfilled dreams, the frustrated talents of our ancestors are manifested in the rebelliousness of these black sheep seeking fulfilment. The genealogical tree, by inertia, will want to continue to maintain the castrating and toxic course of its trunk, which makes the task of our sheep a complex and conflicting work.

However, who would bring new flowers to our tree if it were not for them? Who would create new branches? Without them, the unfulfilled dreams of those who supported the tree generations ago would die buried beneath their own roots.

Let no one cause you to doubt; take care of your rarity as the most precious flower of your tree.

You are the dream of all your ancestors."*

"*Kuroi hitsuji*. Black sheep", said Kunikaze. "I guess it means *tsumahajiki*.

"I don't know that word," I said.

"To throw someone out of a group."

"Yes. But the black sheep is the *person*. *Tsumahajiki* is the action."

"No, it's the person. There is no more direct translation, I guess. "

"Hm, interesting."

"Did you go to the psychologist?"

"Psychiatrist."

"Same, same."

"No, a psychologist is not the same as a psychiatrist."

"What's the difference?"

"A psychiatrist can prescribe medication. A psychologist can't. But my psychiatrist cannot prescribe medication in Japan."

"So he is a psychologist."

"No."

"Oh."

It was typical for Kunikaze that he did not ask how the session went. He stayed away from difficult subjects. He reminded me of Mum in that way.

*Black Sheep by Bert Hellinger.

4

Place two: The Jewish quarter of Amsterdam

At the beginning of the session, Vossberg asked me what I liked about myself. I stared at my feet for a long time, pondering the question. I was never asked such a thing and was unsure what to say. I was wearing eggplant-coloured boots. I had a mustard-coloured pair too.

"Come on, give it a try," said Vossberg.

"My shoes," I said, "I like my shoes."

"Okay, this needs improvement," he said. What's your place today?"

"The Jewish quarter of Amsterdam."

"Associating thoughts, feelings and images about this place, please?"

"A leaking, leaning attic apartment. My unhappy mum. My sagging socks. Our neighbours: Ida and Moos. The bread tricycle of Moos, the man that never slept. Like Opa, who also slept very little, something happened to him during the war. Talking about the war was taboo. The first studio of my father with its paint-stained tables and etching press. The cutting of the hair of Jan Two; a shocking event. The Jazz bands that Dad played in that came to the attic to rehearse. The smell of beer, the smoke of cigarettes, the sound of laughter and Jazz... Mum's blooming skirts, her pointy bras. Her dangling earrings... Her lipstick in the golden shaft... The girl called Mirror and my loss of her. The red dot on my nose. The shame and the embarrassment over who I was.

My toys in the kitchen drawer... The place where Mum betrayed Dad with Jan One while Dad was in isolation with jaundice. The roof upon which they had watched the full moon. What could he give her that Dad could not? The cutting of Mum's hair. The selling of Mum's hair. This was the second shocking hair-event... Dad's absentmindedness... How the attic was lined with Masonite and leaked when it rained...

"So you were raised by two narcissist children in a leaky attic in the Jewish Quarter of Amsterdam. You did not have toys. You played with things from the kitchen drawer. You also played with your reflection in the mirror. You resembled a small, lonely animal. You had no one to play with. No wonder you collapsed when you saw that girl in the movie *The Taste of Water*. She resembled you!"

I was astounded by that statement. I felt a sharp betrayal towards Mum and Dad. It could not have been that bad, could it?

"My parents took care of me; the carers of the girl in the movie didn't."

"Did they?"

"What do you mean?"

"Did they take care of you?"

"I wanted to say "yes, of course".

Instead, I said: "No, they didn't really."

I put my face in my hands and wept. "I don't know. I don't know."

"What don't you know?"

"I don't know if they took care of me."

Vossberg let me cry. It did not stop. The man had the patience of an oyster.

"Why are you crying?" he asked eventually.

"I am so confused."

"I think you are crying because your parents did not take care of you. Based on your stories, I think they were *both* narcissists. Narcissists suck the life out of their children and leave a trail of destruction and pain."

I looked up from my numb hands, which were wet with tears. "Really?"

"Yes."

I had to process this. Waves of guilt washed through me while I pondered this possibility. I pictured Narcissus at the pond, admiring his image. A strong urge to defend Mum and Dad arose inside of me.

"But they fed me, clothed me, provided a roof..."

"From a psychiatric perspective, narcissistic parents negatively impact their children in various serious ways. Narcissists have an inflated sense of self and a lack of empathy, which results in them prioritising their own needs and wants over those of their children. This can lead to them being emotionally abusive, criticising and belittling their children, and manipulating and controlling them. Such behaviour makes the children feel drained, as they constantly try to meet the parent's expectations, which is impossible. Growing up in such an environment harms the child's self-esteem, leads to feelings of inadequacy, and negatively impacts their ability to form healthy relationships in the future..."

"Stop," I said. I blew air through the lips that had just betrayed Mum and Dad. I could not bear Vossberg agreeing with me. "They were decent people."

"Were they?"

Mum and Dad not being decent people. This was a new and terrifying perspective. I felt Dad stir within me in protest. He said: *You did not resemble the girl in the movie in her dirty, torn clothes. This psychiatrist is fucking with your mind. We took care of you. We loved you. Psychiatry is nonsense. See where it got you?*

I repeated this to Vossberg.

"Really?"

"They had many friends."

"Who?"

"My parents."

"And you? Did you have many friends?"

"No."

"Who are we talking about here?"

"Me."

"Exactly," said Vossberg. "Children who grow up with two narcissistic parents face a challenging and often damaging childhood. In such households, the needs and wants of the parents are the only ones that matter. The children are seen as mere extensions of the parents rather than as individuals with their own needs. These children struggle to develop a sense of self, as they are constantly told that their thoughts and feelings are unimportant. The fact that you don't know what you like about yourself tells me that all this applies to you. Children of narcissists feel a constant need to please their parents, leading to a lack of autonomy and feelings of being trapped. This results in low self-esteem, anxiety and depression. The constant criticism and belittling harm their ability to form healthy relationships and trust others. They struggle with intimacy and find it difficult to open up to others or to seek help. In such an environment, the children struggle to form a stable sense of identity, as they are never allowed to express themselves freely or to develop their interests. They feel like they live in a vacuum without meaningful connections or opportunities. In short, growing up with two narcissistic parents is a deeply damaging experience that has long-lasting effects on a child's mental and emotional well-being. Now tell me, is this you or not?"

I looked at him. He was a small grey man sitting in a grubby old church office in a foreign land where he could not prescribe medication. I suppressed a strong urge to tell him just that, to tear him down, to humiliate him, like Dad would have done if he were here... I could feel Dad take hold of my thoughts. *He is a fraud.*

Instead, I said, almost against my will: "Yes, that is me."

That day, I left Vossberg's office feeling broken beyond repair. If parents could do this to their children, what hope did I have of getting better? Would I always feel this way? For the rest of my life? Because my parents were both narcissists? Were my relationships dysfunctional? I thought of Kunikaze. We were like two strangers living in the same apartment. We had nothing in common but food. But wasn't that the attraction? Nothing made sense any longer. I thought of Flaxen and my children. My relationship with them had failed. They were in Europe, and I was here, in Japan. Was I a narcissist, too? This thought brought on another wave of fear. I also thought of Flo. Yes, when I thought of her, I could see clearly how neglected she was by both Mum and Dad. Was I neglected like that, too? Flo was the child of another man; I was not. I resembled Dad. Flo looked like hers: Jan, Dad's best friend. What about Lilibeth? Mum had had her on her hip all day. She adored Lilibeth. I should ask Vossberg about that next time. But was it not *me* who had said Mum wore Lilibeth like a brooch? Was Lilibeth merely a beautiful accessory to Mum? Mum had always put much importance into how we looked. She had been a show-off child herself. Pretty. Blonde. Blue-eyed. Maybe she did not know any better... Maybe Opa and Oma van R had been narcissists too... My hands acutely went numb.

Vossberg explained it in the next session: "The symptom of numbness or tingling in the hands, known as peripheral neuropathy, is not directly caused by being raised by narcissistic parents. However, the stress and emotional trauma that results from growing up with narcissistic parents can impact physical health and exacerbate or trigger symptoms of various medical conditions, including peripheral neuropathy. Chronic stress, anxiety, and depression, common in people with narcissistic parents, can cause changes in the body's stress response system, leading to physical symptoms such as numbness and tingling in the hands. A constant state of alertness and tension leads to muscle tension and compression of nerves in the neck, arms, and hands, resulting in peripheral neuropathy symptoms. But just to be sure, I want you to go to the hospital and undergo what they call a *human dock*. All functions of your physique are tested. I think you could benefit from this. I cannot write you a referral, so you must pay for it in full or get a referral from a Japanese doctor."

I thought about the cigar smoking, Amway selling White Coat.

"I'll give it a miss," I said. "I believe you when you say my symptoms are psychosomatic. It is terrifying that the mind can do this to a person. I went through a *human dock* not long ago at considerable expense. I'll bring you the results next time."

"The mind is a powerful thing," answered Vossberg. "But if it has the power to make you this unwell, it must have the power to make you better, too, doesn't it?"

"Have you seen such recoveries?"

"Oh, yes, many. Recovering from the effects of having two narcissistic parents is challenging and complex, but it is entirely possible. I hope to provide you with a safe and supportive environment to process and heal from emotional trauma. I can help you develop coping strategies and improve your self-esteem and self-worth.

Being able to share your experiences and feelings with others also provides a sense of validation and relief. You must have instinctively known this because, as you say, you are good at friendship.

Taking care of your physical and emotional health is crucial in recovery. This includes engaging in enjoyable, relaxing exercise, meditation, or other hobbies.

And by all means: Set boundaries! You have put much distance between your narcissistic parents and yourself. Well done! You must have known instinctively that this was a good thing to do.

We will work on self-reflection and self-compassion. Developing a positive and compassionate view of yourself helps counteract the negative self-image that your narcissistic parents have instilled in you. This involves practising self-reflection, learning to recognise and challenge negative thoughts, and being kind and understanding towards yourself. You could seek support from a support group. Joining a support group for individuals who have experienced similar challenges can provide a sense of community, validation, and understanding. I, unfortunately, do not know of any such groups in Tokyo, but we could try to start one. Does that sound attractive to you?"

"No, not at all."

"It's important to remember that recovery is a process. It takes time and patience. With proper support, overcoming the effects of having two narcissistic parents is possible. So, let's pick up where we have left. Continue to tell me the story. We were in an attic in the Jewish quarter of Amsterdam. Have you said enough about this place, or is there more?"

I thought about it.

"No, we can move on."

Mexico Delight

Kunikaze had insisted I'll go out to have dinner with him. I had been reluctant.

"I can't drink alcohol, Kukikaze. Please don't make me. And it shouldn't be noisy."

We took a cab to Mexico Delight in Kunitachi.

They made tacos in the shape of a bowl with one raised side. Beans, meats, sauces, olives, guacamole, and sour cream were piled high against the raised part.

"Holy guacamole," I said, seeing the forty-centimetre-high food towers.

"What?"

"Holy guacamole."

"What does that mean?"

"It's a joke."

"Explain!"

"But then it's not funny anymore."

"Why not?"

I sighed. How do you explain "holy guacamole" to a Japanese person? "It's an exclamation," I said. Something like: "Eeeeeeeeh." Or like, "Holy shit".

"But you said: "guacamole".

"Yes, because that rhymes with holy."

"Why is that funny?"

"It isn't anymore."

"Oh."

5

Place three: Etersheim, the Netherlands

Vossberg began the session with an analysis: "You talked about infidelity. The impact of infidelity by a parent on children is far-reaching. It causes emotional distress. The child is angry, sad, confused, and fearful. Infidelity erodes the trust that children have in their parents. The child is exposed to conflict and instability, which is stressful and disruptive. Infidelity shakes a child's sense of security and stability. She may feel shame or self-blame. Do you recognise yourself in any of this?"

"Well, duh, yeah."

"How did you find out about your mother's affair?"

"She told us about it."

"When?"

"When I was about twelve and Flo about ten."

"What did she tell you?"

"That Dad had been sick for a long time; he was in isolation, and she had felt like going out. She'd attended a school reunion with Jan. They had climbed on the roof. There was a full moon. Jan had kissed her. From one thing came another. They had "done" it in the gutter."

"Unbelievable."

"What? Infidelity. Does it not happen frequently?"

"No, the fact that she told you at that age and how she told it. A narcissist! Tell me of your next place."

"Place number three is the parsonage next to the church in Etersheim, a tiny village in the North of the Netherlands."

"Associating thoughts and images, please."

"My grandparents from my father's side. The long grass. The pebble path to the church. The cast iron gate. The windswept landscape at the Inland Sea. The farmer who used a VW Beetle as a horse cart. The cigars of Uncle Arne. The piano. The name 'Rik Schipper'. Oma and her corset. The way she held me in her lap."

"Why did you call him 'uncle'?" asked Vossberg.

"My real grandfather was in prison. He had worked with and for the Germans during the War. He worked at 4711, an *eau de cologne* factory. He had plenty of eau de cologne to trade for food while the rest of the country was starving. He was a traitor. No one in the family wants to talk about him. I met him only once when I was about sixteen. That must all have had quite an impact on Dad."

"Your drive to defend your dad is strong," observed Vossberg. "I wish you would have such a drive to defend yourself."

I thought about Flaxen and his mother and how I had not defended myself against them when they took my children away. Hot tears streamed down my cheeks immediately. I told Vossberg about it.

"You did not defend yourself. I bet your sense of self is absent, too?"

Speechless, I nodded.

"And now you're living with some guy who *does* take out the trash."

"Some guy?" I retorted. "Kunikaze is a decent man."

"Sorry," said Vossberg, "that's not what I meant."

"But you're right. I live with a random guy."

"Why?"

"Because love frightens the hell out of me. Because I think that love does not exist."

"You do not love your children?"

"I love my children more than anything. That's why I had to let them go."

"Explain."

"I am afraid that I will have a damaging effect on them. Perhaps I am a narcissist myself."

"Let's test you for that."

"Is that even possible?"

"I'll bring a test next time. Continue your memory chain for now."

"Okay: vegetable gardens, the smell of meat cooking, my grandparents singing hymns in the kitchen…the church where my aunt Tran played the organ. The dogs and cats. There was a cat who could swim. She swam in the creeks. How strange! And the parsonage; that house. That wonderful, wonderful house."

"Is it still in the family?"

"Oh no. Not for a long time. Oma and Uncle Arne are buried in the little graveyard beside the church. But they moved to an awful new housing estate in an awful new neighbourhood when they were older, and both died soon afterwards. They resembled two animals in a cage in that new, proper little house. Oh God, I argued with them there. They disagreed with how I looked, the hippy-style, when I was about fifteen. I was wearing a wooden cross. They found that offensive. We had never argued. They spoke the language of love."

"And your parents? Did they speak the language of love?"

I paused. Almost against my will, my head shook, no.

"So, what is the difference between your parents' "love" and those 'who speak the language of love?'"

"There is a natural quality to the love they display, those that speak the language of love. Their default position is love."

"And that is not the case with your parents?"

"No. Their love is conditional."

"There you said it. What were the conditions?"

"For Mum, we had to look good and 'proper'. For Dad, we had to perform well and be talented. He praised me because I could sing and draw. Flo could not sing in tune. He put her down for it. Later, when I drew a lot in my teens, he said I had to stop drawing because I was no longer good at it. I was terrified of his judgements. It was all about praise and blame. His blame was devastating."

"Would you say he praised you for what suited *him* somehow?"

"Dad was only interested in those aspects of us which aligned with his interests. I was interested in horse riding, ballet and gymnastics. I never even got the gear to do it properly. He actively discouraged me from engaging in these activities. He called them 'right-wing hobbies'. He changed his tune completely when he met Agata, but that is another story I will come to soon enough."

"Your mum, she went along with this?"

"Mum," I said, "Mum seemed to be there only to do the housekeeping and the cooking. To be a slave. And she did it willingly. She did not have a say in anything. She did not even try. All she wanted was a vase of flowers on the table, nice clothes, pretty pottery and furniture. She was a good cook but always made a little too little. It was because she was a small eater, I guess."

"Everything you describe screams' narcissists', can't you see?"

"I can with my brain. I cannot *feel* it."

"That's only natural," said Vossberg. "You have only recently learned that you are the child of two narcissists."

"I am so afraid that I will never recover."

"You will recover. I will stay with you as long as it takes."

"You speak the language of love," I said, "and we're not even related."

"Sometimes it's like that."

"Dad threatened to throw us out of the car at the side of the highway in France if we did not behave. He slowed down the car and turned into a resting bay while we howled with fear."

"She did not stop him, your mum?"

"Nope."

"I am glad you can now find examples of narcissistic behaviour. I do not have to point them out anymore. This stream of thought and associating seems to work for you."

"As long as I bind it to places where I have lived, it works."

"Good."

Garlic Mansion

"Shan, there's a new restaurant in Nakano. Garlic Mansion. Let's go," said Kunikaze.

"Can't we order something?"

"Have you been outside today?"

"No, but…"

"Come on." He turned my shoes around in the *genkan*, so that I could slip into them.

Garlic had just reached Tokyo. It wasn't used often at all in Japan. The Japanese did not like the smell of it. But it seemed to have become trendy lately, like cheese.

We went to Nakano by train. I tried not to feel dizzy.

The restaurant was too noisy to my liking, but I was sick of explaining to Kunikaze again that noise made my vertigo worse. Kunikaze thought every day that I was miraculously cured, it seemed. Or maybe he thought I should fake it until I made it. He preferred not to talk about my "condition" at all.

There was a long line in front of the restaurant. As we shuffled forwards in the line, we could see energetic chefs in *happi* coats handling hot woks as if they were jugglers. Once inside, we were led to an enormous circular counter behind which *hibachi* fires hissed and crackled, oil sizzled, and food was tossed in the air and caught on a plate, emitting the smell of roasted garlic. Excited customers occupied all stools. I picked at my food, wishing I was part of the hustle and bustle, but I felt separated from it as if I was behind glass.

"Don't you like it? You love garlic."

Shit! This is why he had brought me here. I was a foreigner. So I liked garlic. I did not belong. So I liked garlic.

"I have difficulty eating," I explained once again.

"But you love garlic."

"I do."

"So eat."

"What about you?"

"I don't like garlic."

"Why did we go here then?"

"Because you like garlic."

"What are you eating?"

"They have special dishes without garlic for people who don't like garlic. There's a separate menu for those."

"Very Japanese indeed, a garlic restaurant with a separate menu for people who do not like garlic."

"Very considerate."

"Very considerate," I agreed and hated myself for being sarcastic.

6

Place four: Hoorn, the Netherlands

Vossberg began with a reminder: "Children who do not receive unconditional love from their parents experience negative psychological effects; feelings of low self-esteem, worthlessness, and insecurity. They struggle with trust issues and have difficulty forming healthy relationships later in life. These children struggle to regulate emotions and engage in unhealthy coping mechanisms like substance abuse. Is this you?"

"Ehm, I think it is clear it is. I'm pretty fucked up. I feel numb like a serial killer most of the time."

"Why do you use the term "serial killer" and not, for example, "statue".

"Because the numbness has an evil quality."

"Evil?"

"A scary quality."

"I see. And why do you think that is?"

"I don't know. You are the expert, you tell me!"

"The answers are in *you*, not in me," said Vossberg. "Look inside."

"I don't know how to do that."

"You do. You don't know yet that you do. Now, tell me your place."

A place called Hoorn. Also, in the North. "The home of Oma and Opa van R, my maternal grandparents."

"Associated thoughts, feelings and images, please."

"Their lovely large, organised house. The Persil factory. The smell of soap powder. A giant stuffed monkey. A black doll with blue eyes. Absurd! The way Opa spoke about Germans and the sound of boots in the streets, and the Jews... The pretend-shooting of rows of Jews against a wall while Oma ushered us, children, away from the *jenever-fuelled* scene."

"Did they speak the language of love?"

"Yes, oh yes. Both were extremely fond of us. They loved all children. I do not understand how Mum became a narcissist with such parents."

"You said your mother was a child on display herself."

"Yes, because she and her sister were so pretty, especially when together; one blonde, the other one dark. Both had large blue eyes and very long plats. Ribbons in their hair. Pretty dresses..."

"Well, there you've got your answer."

"But that in itself is not damaging. Mum's sister is a lovely woman. She has gone through something similar to what I am currently going through. The same symptoms."

"How interesting."

"Mum's sister also speaks the language of love. We have been exchanging letters. She writes to me often. Oh, I feel terrible towards my mum. I feel like inviting her and saying I am sorry."

"Sorry for...?"

"For always listening to Dad. For never protecting her against him and his insanity."

"Was that your task? As a child? Her task was to protect *you*."

"I know, but I *feel* this way. I always took his side, even when he did terrible things to her."

"Nothing prevents you from inviting her to Japan. First, you must get stronger."

"I may do just that."

"Give me some more associative thought around your maternal grandparent's home..."

"Two teenage boys, my uncles. They did nothing but sleep ... Their electric train...their dinky toys...the smell of soap everywhere...the cleanliness and order... it makes me feel safe even thinking about it. They took me on several holidays in their caravan. It was the same there: order, cleanliness, the smell of soap, and love and eh... a slight nagging boredom."

"Maybe it was too safe?"

"Maybe. Even the tea towels were ironed, even while on holiday...I think there was a TV in the caravan because Opa could not live without his soccer. He'd scream at the screen."

"So, there was some friction too?"

"Yes, there were the remnants of the war and other stuff that I did not understand... They did not talk about things but put painful stuff away... Who knows what their demons were... Opa had to hide during the war. They also hid Jews, I think. So, the fact that Dad's father was in jail for being a traitor must have been difficult for them. Or maybe they didn't even know it. They did their best to like Dad. They had his art on their walls: a Rembrandtesque etching and a small abstract oil painting. The style of these paintings was very different from the rest of their paintings: a thickly painted still-life of flowers and a scene of a wooden caravan in a forest. They still have these pieces, although they moved to a slightly smaller house and later to an apartment... Everywhere that same clean, orderly atmosphere, the paintings... and the crockery in a wooden cupboard...The Sunday roasts... Opa carving the meat. My memories of them are loving, perhaps the most loving I have experienced. The lamplight felt protective and warm... But I lost them early, although not to death, but to Agata, of whom more later..."

"This Agata, she seemed to have caused you pain."

"I will come to her later. I was eleven when she entered my life, so we'll get to her soon."

"Anything else connected to your maternal grandparent's home?"

"Friendships with other girls. There were always other girls when we went away in the caravan. We stayed at camping sites. Opa put his feet up in a striped chair under the awning while Oma pottered around, or should I say 'slaved' while I went to the playground. I met other girls there. Oma encouraged these friendships… I remember a bicycle tournament with lances on bicycles instead of horses. I vaguely remember a girl I befriended. It is not the person I remember but the quality of our friendship. Safe and warm. I was tormented at home; at Opa and Oma's, I was not. Memory is a strange thing."

"It is," agreed Vossberg. "It is not accurate at all."

"Does that mean that everything I am telling you is not true? It often feels that way."

"No, you are telling me *your* truth."

"Subjective truth, is that a thing?"

"In psychiatry, it is. And probably in the world too. There may be no objective truth at all. We don't know that."

"Is that why I feel like a fraud when I tell you all this?"

"No, that's because you have no confidence, no self-worth. For you, truths of others are right, and yours is wrong."

This was a startling observation. I had to pause and think. Was this true?

"Your father speaks through you because you have not learned to speak for yourself, "Vossberg clarified.

I placed my hand on my hot forehead.

"I'm thirty years old and don't know who I am. How embarrassing!"

I covered my mouth with my hand as if to stifle a scream.

"Nothing is embarrassing about it," said Vossberg. "Some people never grow into themselves because it is simply too painful."

"Why is becoming oneself painful?"

"Because we slash through conditioning. That hurts."

"Why does it have to be that way."

"I don't know. It is just the way it is."

Tofu Den

"Let's go, let's go, let's go!" Kunikaze was already in the *genkan* turning my shoes around.

I put down my paintbrush and dragged myself to the hallway.

"Let's go to a Japanese-style place then, please, Kunikaze. Something quiet and without stimuli."

"Tofu Den."

"Yes!"

We had been to Tofu Den before. Everything was made of a pale kind of wood there, the same colour as the tatami.

"Can we take a taxi and not the train, please?"

"Sure."

We stepped through the *noren*. The sliding door opened silently. Before us stretched a field of tatami, seemingly to the horizon. We removed our shoes and were led to a low, smooth wooden table. We sat on beige cushions and extended our legs in the pit under the table. The pit was heated. The walls had the colour of sand, and straw was mixed in the plaster. The low ceilings were made of wood. A long wall of paper sliding doors stretched to our right. There were no knicknacks or other decorations—even no plants.

"Oh, this is nice."

Kunikaze looked at me anxiously to see if I was being sarcastic. I hated what my "condition", as he called it, was doing to him.

I could not read the menu because the kanji were too specialised. Kinikaze read it to me. The Spirit of the Fox increasingly led me to avoid meat and fish. We settled for a monastery meal for two.

The waiters were dressed in light brown kimono. They served the dishes while seated on their knees at the short end of the table. Wooden trays held many small bowls and plates, all meticulously decorated with

Japanese food. The food was based on the principles of simplicity and harmony. Dishes were prepared with balance in five different colours and flavours. Nutritional balance was central to the preparation of these dishes. Nothing went to waste when preparing them. Every last piece of each ingredient was somehow incorporated into the meal. Garlic, onion and other pungent flavours were avoided. There was tofu and *abura-age;* friend soybean curd. *Goma-dofu;* sesame tofu, *koya-dofu,* dried tofu, *yuba;* soy milk film, *fu;* wheat gluten, and marbled *konnyaku;* rum root cakes, on a stick. There were seaweed dishes with *konbu;* kelp, *wakame;* sea green, *nori*, and *hijiki*. Wild plants such as *warabi;* fiddlehead fern, and *zenmai;* flowering fern, were used in abundance.

This was the type of food I could eat. It pleased Kunikaze that this was so.

I closed my eyes while drinking from the cloudy miso soup. Small, slippery mushrooms popped into my mouth.

We ate in silence, not only with our mouths but also our eyes.

I picked up a square piece of fluffy omelette. It melted in my mouth.

"I'm so glad you can enjoy that," said Kunikaze.

7

Place five: Gorinchem, the Netherlands

Vossberg began the session. "The presence of supportive and caring grandparents can positively influence and counteract some of the negative effects of narcissistic parents. Ultimately, the child's success will depend on a complex interplay of factors, and the presence of caring grandparents alone is not guaranteed to ensure success. However, their support can provide a foundation for the child's well-being and future success."

"So there is hope."

Vossberg smiled.

"Well, I'm afraid that hope will soon be crushed."

"Where are we this time?"

"Place Five: A modern apartment in Gorinchem, in the Middle West, where my sister Flo was mostly ignored, and I bonded further with Dad.

"Images, thoughts and feelings, please...."

"The place where Mum's crying intensified. Or was that even earlier? I was Daddy's girl entirely. How he read to me, sang with me, ran to me, disciplined me. How he loved me and how I loved him back. Dad permeated everything, while Mum was in tears at the slightest until she had Lilibeth. How Lilibeth made Mum whole again and how Mum wore her like a brooch. How Mum lied about a birthday present from Dad. How there had been a neighbour who was not a breadwinner, a kind man who had offered to watch over Flo. Mum had not taken up his offer and had left Flo alone. The hook on the bedroom door and our tantrums when locked up."

Your mum left her baby alone?"

"All the time!"

"You were locked up?"

"All the time."

"Your mum lied about a birthday present?"

"Yes. Dad had given her an expensive camera with several lenses. Someone else had given her what we called a "babydoll", a nightie made out of lace; it was pink with shorts and short sleeves, all quite see-through. The presents were laid out on a table. When Oma V asked what Dad had given her, Mum did not grab the camera, but the nighty and held it against her body. "This," she said. "Isn't it cute?""

"She did that in front of her kids?"

"And right in front of Dad too. We did not say a word. Dad did not say anything, either. It was bewildering."

"Telling lies in front of the children is known to hurt."

"Gawd. Does it ever stop?"

"Yes," said Vossberg. "Remember?"

"Everything passes."

"Everything passes."

"Are your symptoms getting less?"

"Hm. Maybe. A tiny little bit. I don't know. My days are pretty rough."

"And how is your man taking it?"

"Kunikaze? He does not get involved."

"How is that even possible."

"He's Japanese."

"Meaning?"

"He is not into feelings. Hey, how come the Japanese don't seem to suffer from all this childhood trauma? They seem so into equanimity."

"Oh yes, psychiatry in Japan is very different from Western psychiatry in many ways. Japanese culture has a unique perspective on mental health and illness, influencing how psychiatric disorders are diagnosed and treated. The Japanese classification of mental disorders, the Diagnostic and Statistical Manual of Mental Disorders-Japanese Version (DSM-IV-J), includes some disorders not included in the Western DSM. Japanese psychiatrists take a holistic approach to mental health, considering the individual's social and cultural context and psychological symptoms. Japanese psychiatrists often use different treatments for mental health conditions than those used in the West, such as herbal remedies, acupuncture, and traditional Japanese therapies like *Shinnō*.

"What is *Shinnō*?"

"It is based on the idea that disruptions in energy flow within the body cause mental and emotional problems. It typically involves guided meditation, visualisation, and deep breathing exercises. It may also involve physical movements, music, and aromatherapy. While it is not widely recognised or used in Western psychiatric practices, it is an important aspect of traditional Japanese medicine."

"Should I do any of these?"

"No. Not now, anyway. It is important to note that *shinnō* should not be used as a substitute for evidence-based psychiatric treatment and should only be used in conjunction with other psychiatric treatments under the guidance of a qualified mental health professional. We are not there yet. Instead, I am going to give you the narcissism test."

I filled out the forty questions on the form.

Vossberg added up the answers.

"You're thirty per cent narcissist. That's twenty per cent less than the average U.S. president, thirteen per cent less than the average reality TV star and three per cent less than the average U.S. adult."

"Isn't that high?"

"No, it's quite low. Everyone scores some points."

"What would Mum and Dad typically score then?"

"Sixty to eighty, perhaps. But that is just guesswork."

"Dad would never do a test like this anyway."

"Of course not."

"Yeah, right."

"When a parent lies to a child, and the child realises it," said Vossberg, "it has several negative effects. The child has difficulty trusting the parent in the future and questions their honesty. Children rely on their parents for accurate information, so a parent's lie causes confusion and disrupts the child's sense of security and stability. Children feel hurt or betrayed by a parent's lie, leading to anger, sadness, and anxiety. Children learn by example, so if a parent models dishonesty, the child struggles with being truthful."

"Strange!? I said, "I've always thought that we were "special", that we were "better". Instead, our family is dysfunctional as hell."

"Every child thinks their family is special. Waking up from that illusion is painful. In your case, the discrepancy between dream and reality is huge. But be glad you're waking up from it at all. Some people never do; *most* people never do."

"I feel like I'm losing more and more. Is the therapy supposed to make one feel that way?"

"It usually gets worse and then better."

"How much longer do I need?"

"Difficult to say. A couple of years?"

"Years?" I was taken aback.

"Yes."

"Holy guacamole!"

Washoku

Restaurant Washoku used Japan's seasonal produce grown in seas and rivers, on mountains and land. It was named after the style of food it served. Meals consisted of rice, soup, side dishes, and pickles. The most important ingredient was the dashi broth. It was this soup, made by drawing out the umami from ingredients such as *katsuobushi* (dried bonito flakes), *kombu* (kelp), and *niboshi* (dried baby anchovies or sardines), which provided the fundamental flavours of the cuisine. They used fermented condiments such as soy sauce and miso. Their tempura was epic and served with five different salts.

The food was presented beautifully. A delicate square of pistachio *tofu* was served with tiny purple *shiso* flowers and fresh *wasabi*. Pumpkin *tofu* was plated alongside *namafu*, wrapped in bamboo and a piece of *inarizushi*; a fried *tofu* pouch filled with *sushi* rice and topped with green tea salt.

The broth contained chilled sesame tofu, tender miso-glazed eggplant, and yuba (tofu skin).

"Have you heard of macrobiotics?" asked Kunikaze.

"Eeew."

"It's supposed to be healthy."

"My father used to cook macrobiotic food. It was disgusting."

"I heard there is a good macrobiotic restaurant in Hajuioji. Shall we go?"

"No. I prefer this style. White rice, traditional, bland."

8

Place six: Arkel, the Netherlands

Vossberg was quiet at the beginning of the session. He was able to bear very long silences. I was less good at that, so eventually, I began:

"Location Six: A place called Arkel. A backward place. About five kilometres away from Gorinchem."

"Thoughts, feelings, images; associations?"

"A small village, a white-washed country house. Ground. Soil. Grass. A hazelnut tree. Frogs. A dike. Rivers are about to burst their banks. Quicksand. Reeds. The house is too big for Mum to keep clean. We get a cleaner: Nel. She knits clothes for our Barbie dolls. She is the first fat person I know. She speaks the language of love. I can still feel the embraces in her soft woollen jumpers. It is in this house that Flo goes troppo. Although we've both been given a room, finally apart, she has to sleep in my room because she is scared."

"Scared of what?"

"Men."

"Men?"

"Men that climb through the windows. Men that lie under the beds. Men that stand behind the curtains. Men. Men. Men..."

"How many men did Flo know?"

"Dad, Dad's friends..."

"And she's scared of men! What happened to her?"

"I don't know. I found it super annoying at the time."

"Annoying?"

"I'm as bad as Mum and Dad regarding Flo. I didn't like her and didn't want to share with her."

"You didn't like your sister?"

"I know, it's fucked up, but no, I did not like her. I felt no affinity with her at all."

"Why do you think that was?"

"Gosh. It was an animalistic thing, almost like dogs not liking each other. I don't know what it was. The wrong scent? We did not gel. It is like that to this day. I would rather not have her around."

"I see."

"I played a game called "lovers" with some girls from school. I guess it was our first experience of arousal. We climbed into bed under the blankets and kissed. This later led to me being bullied at school."

"You have quite some traumas in your basket. Tell me about the bullying. Was it physical?"

"Mental and physical. Pushing, shoving... packs of kids... letters. I never told Mum and Dad. I involved a teacher. Mr Roll. Mr Roll spoke the language of love. He protected me. But the letters continued arriving, even after we had moved to the next place. They somehow got a hold of my new address."

"You moved around a lot."

"We did, for Dad's job. We did not live in that awful village for long. Two years tops, I think... Dad was offered a teaching position at an art academy. I experienced bliss with a boy bobbing on the river Maas in truck tyres, away from Mum and Flo and ever closer to Dad. He had taken me on holiday, and I met this boy, and we gelled. His name was Ron, and he taught me never to say "negro".

I also recall how Dad read *Kees, de jongen* (Kees, The Boy) to me, a Dutch book for children, and how he wept while reading it."

"Your Dad wept."

"Yes, he frequently did when moved by art. Later, we wept together."

"I see."

We were silent for a long time; each lost in our thoughts.

For the next session, Vossberg had prepared his analyses:

"Ongoing bullying has a long-lasting impact on a child. It leads to physical, emotional, and psychological problems, including low self-esteem. Bullied children often feel helpless, worthless, sad, afraid, and insecure, which can develop into depression and anxiety. They may get headaches, stomach aches, and insomnia. They may struggle in school and experience a decline in school performance. They may have thoughts of suicide and may be at an increased risk for self-harm."

"Holy shit."

"How old were you?"

"Ten."

"Is there a pattern arising?"

"There seems to be a lot that Dad and Mum overlooked. They were not very involved. Although we did get our garden plots in the garden in Arkel, they did not do much to help us with the gardening. They just gave us plots. As if we knew what we had to do with them."

"I see."

"I feel crushed with guilt when I say this."

"I understand. As you gain more insight into your situation, this feeling will decrease. How are your other symptoms?"

"I live in a state of permanent vertigo, which is extremely exhausting."

"I'm sorry it is taking so long. Maybe you should ask a Japanese doctor for medication."

"No!"

"Vertigo it is. It will pass."

"It will pass."

"Hey, kiddo," said Vossberg while I walked out the door. "There is a bit of a spring in your step."

I looked at my mustard-yellow lace-up boots.

"It must be my boots; I feel a thousand years old."

"See you in two days."
"I cannot believe what an unwell mind can do."
"You better believe it."
Vossberg waved.
I waved back and stepped into my hellish day.

Sushiko Honten

I was meeting Kunikaze in Ginza.

I tried to go into a department store. I had a lemon in the pocket of my coat. I smelled it when I felt anxiety rising.

I stepped inside. It was quiet and spacious. I walked around a bit, looking at make-up and gloves. I thought about the visits to department stores with Mum when I was little. I took the lemon from my pocket and smelled it. But it was to no avail. Vertigo washed over me. I hurried to the doors.

Being outside was just about bearable.

I called Kunikaze from a public phone. "I'm in front of Matsuya."

"I'll be there in ten minutes."

I held the lemon in my hand, pressed a cut in the peel with my nail and smelled it. It kept the vertigo at bay. Just.

"I feel like trying some sushi," I said when Kunikaze arrived.

"Ah, that's a good sign," he said. "Let's go to Sushiko Honten, then."

It was one of the oldest sushi restaurants in Tokyo; It could be easily missed due to its humble exterior. It was Michelin-starred and expensive. You got your personal sushi chef once inside. Kunikaze made a reservation on a public phone. There were only ten seats around a wooden counter where you could see the chefs at work. Miraculously, there were two seats available only an hour later.

The chefs decided on the courses, *omakase*-style. You never knew what to expect, but regardless of what was served, you could be sure it was spectacular. They specialise in traditional *edo-mae-zushi*.

"Would you try some sake?" asked Kunikaze, always keen to share his alcohol cravings.

"No, I can't Kunikaze, sorry."

We ordered sushi and sashimi. Our chef showed off his knife mastery. I was keenly aware of the specialness of the occasion. But I could not *feel* it. I was dead inside like a serial killer. This made me very, very sad.

"Kunikaze chattered away cheerfully. He desperately wanted to cheer me up. He drank about a litre of hot sake and was too drunk and flustered to take the train. He fell asleep in the taxi.

9

Place seven: Pont Aven, Bretagne, France

"Where are you taking us today?" asked Vossberg.

"I don't know if I can go on."

"What do you mean?"

"I can't bear it anymore."

"Do you mean that you are thinking of killing yourself?"

The directness of his question shocked me.

"I have to ask this," he said. "I need to know. Are you thinking of killing yourself?"

"What is my quality of life? None! I live with constant vertigo. Why?"

"I don't know," said Vossberg. "But if you are thinking of killing yourself, we must talk about that and nothing else."

"I am thinking about it quite a bit."

"I see. Did you make any practical plans?"

"No."

"It is just a reoccurring thought?"

"Yes. Well, one time, when I was home alone the other day, I took a knife from the block in the kitchen and looked at it."

"Just looked at it?"

"Yes. I held it to see if I had the urge to do something with it."

"Did you feel that urge?"

"No. I put it back after a while, feeling stupid."

"Well done. You see, this is how it works: if you get suicidal, I cannot treat you any longer. You'll need medication. And I cannot prescribe any."

"I know; it won't happen again."

"I need your word on that."

"You have my word."

"Call me if you feel the urge to do something stupid and cannot resist. Even if it is in the middle of the night."

"Okay."

"This too will pass."

"This too will pass."

"Where will you take us today?"

"Pont Aven, Bretagne, France."

"What are your associated thoughts, feelings and images around this place?"

"Summer holidays each year. Paradise. Dad had bought a car. One of the first Citroëns, a two-horsepower. It was yellow."

"I remember that car. A small convertible. Thin as a cookie box."

"We were in awe of it. Dad's holidays were long because he was a teacher. They did not fight that much, Mum and Dad, when we were going places. They were in a good mood or tried to be. The road trips to the camping grounds were long but full of adventures and surprises. We ate French fries with apple sauce and croquettes, otherwise only reserved for birthdays, at the Albert's Corner. We dined and slept in French hotels. We ate French bread with salted butter. We camped at a place called De Roz Pin. There was a gymnastics teacher we adored and many kids to hook up with for the summer. Sea and sun and campfires. Dad and I performed our songs… I made an exceptional friend. Maaike. We were so happy together, floating on our airbeds on the sea, talking about ponies and horses. She was a happy child. It rubbed off on me. I will never forget our barefoot trips to the showers, her sun-streaked long hair, her light blue bikini, and her slender body. She was so special to me.

We chatted over the wall that separated the showers while towelling dry, while walking back to the tent, and while lying in my orange tent..."

"Was she a Dutch child too?"

"Yes. Her family came to De Roz Pin every year too. We practised languages: English and French. We shared an obsession with horses. She was generous. She genuinely wished the best for me. Her kind, light natural generosity was new to me. I thrived in the light of it. That beautiful girl!" I sobbed.

"What happened?"

"First, her father died, and then Agata happened, and I never saw Maaike again."

"I am getting quite curious about who this Agata is."

"Don't. That nightmare will start unfolding soon enough. Let me dwell on these beautiful summers for just a while longer. The crepes we ate from a stall with a giant burner at the top of the stairs to the beach, the games we played at the gymnastic club, the books we read, the promises we made...our collections of seashells, the strolls in the wake of our fathers, who had become friends...Oh, and did I mention Jan? The real father of Flo? He, too, was there with his family every year. Dad lectured the other fathers on art history and architecture. Showed them the churches and paintings... while we begged them for some coins to buy souvenirs, which they gave us absentmindedly... I see the purple flowers of the thistles in the hot sand... the low cottages covered with blue flowers... the blue wooden boats bobbing in the harbours... everything was blue...the sky, the sea...the cobblestone bridges... all caught through the lens of our friendship. It sounds like a cheesy American movie, doesn't it?"

Now it was Vossberg's turn to be shocked. "Why destroy this precious memory with sarcasm?"

Something had shifted between Vossberg and me. A true bond had been forged. He would not abandon me, not if he could help it. How old would he be, I wondered, but I did not dare to ask. He must be in his seventies, easily. He may retire. Where would that leave me? I had many friends but did not speak with them about my ordeal. Only Vossberg knew me. I was deeply known and seen by him. When I stepped out of his door, out of the Baptist Church, into the hustle and bustle of Shibuya's streets, I realised: I did not bond with people; I bonded with *places*. *Tokyo* was the Beloved.

Wafu Spaghetti

"Shall we eat spaghetti?" asked Kunikaze.

"Yes, sure".

I ate a little more now that we went to restaurants almost every evening. Still, I had lost eleven kilos since The Spirit of the Fox visited me and had come to stay.

When in Japan, one should eat spaghetti — specifically, *wafu* spaghetti. "Wafu" refers to something done Japanese-style and can apply to almost anything: Wafu toilets were Japanese-style squatting toilets; a wafu hamburger was made with Japanese flavours. Wafu spaghetti was spaghetti Japanese style. Any Italian would condemn the place. Spaghetti dishes were enriched with umami-laden soy sauce or butter emulsions, replaced Parmesan with seaweed, or switched basil with shiso. Wafu Kokubunji was a multi-story building near Kokubunji Station. It was decorated with lights outside. On the roof were a giant moon and stars. Inside, it looked like a diner, with single guests lined up at a counter, hunched over steaming piles, and couples and families in boots.

Noisy chefs tossed the cooked spaghetti in sizzling pans full of sauce.

It was a result of the *Itameshi Boom*, *itameshi* being a combination of the words Italian and *meshi*, slang for 'meal'. It marked Japan's new obsession with Italian cuisine.

An archetypal style of wafu spaghetti is *tarako*. Hot strands of al dente pasta are tossed with briny pops of *tarako*, salted pollock roe, butter, and soy sauce and garnished with shreds of nori. It was invented by Takayasu Narimatsu, who was introduced to spaghetti by CIA Far East Secretary Paul Bloom, who hired Narimatsu as a server at diplomatic gatherings where foods from around the world were served.

The previous restaurant, *Kabe no Ana,* had only three items on the menu: Spaghetti A (spaghetti with meatballs for 200 yen), Spaghetti B (spaghetti, no meatballs, and extra pasta, 150 yen), and Spaghetti C (regular spaghetti, no meatballs, 100 yen). Then a customer brought in a tin of caviar. The resulting caviar spaghetti was an enormous hit but too expensive, so the more affordable *tarako* was used instead.

Kunikaze ordered the Tarako Spaghetti with a few additions: *shimeji* and *matsutake* mushrooms, green onions and whitefish. I tried the Fiery *Mentaiko S*paghetti, where the pollock was spiced with chillies, in an attempt to *feel* something other but vertigo.

10

Place eight: Amersfoort, the Netherlands

As soon as I had taken my place in the old armchair, Vossberg said: "I've done some research. Anxiety can cause hallucinations. High anxiety and stress levels can lead to sensory distortions, including visual and auditory hallucinations. Anxiety can also cause vertigo. This is because anxiety can affect the inner ear, which is crucial in balance and spatial orientation. Anxiety-induced vertigo can be severe enough to cause nausea and unsteadiness. Stress and anxiety increase muscle tension, which can lead to headaches and neck pain, further exacerbating the symptoms of vertigo. I am rather confident that all your physical symptoms stem from anxiety. We should look into additional therapy or practice for you to find relief. Do you like sports?"

"No," I said, "I've tried to go for runs in my neighbourhood, but I find it boring. Besides, I'm always being stared at. The *gaijin* thing, you know. I did not mind this before I became sick, but now I loathe it."

"I know. Getting older helps. One gets invisible when one ages, even as a *gaijin* in Japan. What about meditation? Would that appeal to you?"

"I thought you could not prescribe medication."

"Meditation!"

"What is meditation?"

"Sitting very still. Observing the mind."

"Yes, that interests me."

"Good. I'll put you in touch with Sato-sensei, a Zen master."

"Oh wow, thank you."

"Do I spot a speck of enthusiasm there?"

I laughed.

"And a little laugh, too, even!"

"I realise that I have not laughed for months. Kunikaze told me."

"Progress!"

"Yes."

I laughed again.

Vossberg seemed pleased. It was an excellent feeling, pleasing him.

"Where would you like to take me today, Kiddo?"

"Place number eight is Amersfoort in the Netherlands."

"Your thought associations, images, feelings?"

"I'd rather cut to the chase. Amersfoort was good to me. I had friends at school and in the neighbourhood. I joined a gymnastics club and rode horses at a nearby farm. We had moved to a large apartment. Flo, Lilibeth and I had our own rooms. Everything was fine for a change, but then Dad…"

I paused.

Vossberg did not say anything. The silence was pregnant with what I was about to reveal.

I felt very guilty when I said: "Dad moved in another woman."

"He did what? He moved in with another woman?"

"No, he fell in love with another woman and moved her in. Her name was Agata."

"Wait a minute…how…"

"First, there was a lot of crying and quarrelling behind the closed kitchen door. It went on for weeks or months; I don't know. Flo and I were terrified. Mum was crying, they were shouting… Flo and I sat in the hallway, listening. We went to Lilibeth's room to make sure she was okay. When the shouting was loud, we covered her ears. Sometimes Mum was throwing things...."

"Good heavens."

"Finally, one evening, Dad came to Flo's room. We were sheltering there because it was farthest from the racket in the kitchen. Lilibeth was asleep in her room. Dad sat on the bed and told us he had fallen in love with another woman but did not want to leave us, so the woman was coming to live with us. We'd known the moment he'd stepped from the bus. He'd been on a school trip for a week. We were at the bus stop to fetch him when he came back. He had been weird. We'd felt it. This is when my life and also Flo's, I am sure, went to shit. Agata indeed moved in, and, as you can imagine, this changed everything."

Vossberg silently chewed his lower lip while he stared at the window.

"Good heavens," he said again. "What happened then?"

"When she arrived, she brought us four doll-shaped pillows that she'd made: two males with erect penises and two females with leather vaginas. The vaginas were lined with chamois leather."

"How old were you?"

"I had just turned eleven, Flo was eight, Lilibeth two."

"I see. And your mother?"

"She went along with it. He'd convinced her in that kitchen, I suppose. Strangely, Agata represented everything he hated: she was a gymnastics teacher. She was Belgian, from a country that Mum hated.

At first, Agata was eager to please. She cooked and cleaned and moved in a lot of stuff. She was good at sewing and made us clothes, curtains, whatnot... She cooked Flemish meals, which made us fat. She was even better at slaving than Mum was. She was stronger than Mum. She had iron hands that were good at wringing out a mop. She ironed sheets with her bare hands."

"And your mother did nothing?"

"No."

Vossberg looked baffled.

"Even you cannot handle it. Think about us."

"Extraordinary. So inappropriate on so many levels."

"Isn't it?"

My guilt was crushing down on me like a rock. The pain in the back of my head and neck intensified. I rubbed it. My hands went numb.

"I feel like throwing up."

Vossberg rose from his armchair and rubbed my back.

I breathed heavily.

"We're entering dangerous territory," he said. "There's but one way to go about it: right through it."

I nodded.

"Agata bullied us for years, Flo and me."

"How?"

"She called us 'spoiled Dutch children' and invented all kinds of drills to toughen us up. Rock climbing, gymnastics, swimming, running, washing dishes, cleaning floors. She was like an army general. She shouted at the sidelines while we exercised."

"And still, your mother did nothing?"

"Nope."

"Neither did your father, I gather?"

"Nope. Our school performance declined."

"Of course."

"Agata had two kids with Dad."

"Why not!" Vossberg said angrily.

"They began favouring these kids over us, except Lilibet, protected by Mum. Lilibeth lived on Mum's hip. Mum let nobody near Lilibeth. In the end, Flo and I had to buy our own food, label it and put it on our own shelves in the fridge. We had to pay part of the water and electricity bills... You know what the worst part is?"

"Tell me!"

"The guilt that I feel telling you this."

"Guilt toward who?"

"Toward them."

"Including Agata?"

"Yes. I wish I could hate them. Instead, I became their little flag bearer, their apologist."

"You were a child."

I rubbed my hands. Then I rubbed my pounding head with my numb hands. Scenes from the past were flooding me. My eyes filled with tears. My throat ached.

"What are you feeling right now?"

I wrinkled my nose to stop the tears.

"My head is about to explode when I think about that time."

"I suggest you embrace that child and give it care. Wrap your arms around her."

I wrapped my arms around my waist and observed how powerless I was. Ripped apart by pain and fear, I sat in the armchair, rocking back and forth slightly.

"Why do I feel that I lie?" I sobbed.

"We are at a crosspoint," Vossberg said. His voice seemed to come from far away.

"You are feeling the pain you were not allowed to feel as a child. That is why it is amplified. Pain amplifies with time if it is neither felt nor examined. Did they not tell you that you felt joy, not pain?"

I nodded, speechless.

"They made you their little soldier, didn't they?"

"I did it willingly. I wrote letters to all those who got angry: the opas and omas, the uncles and aunts, the parents of our friends..." We lost them all eventually. We did not see them for years."

"You went through a war and were forced to like it."

"That's exactly right."

"I bet there was a lot of sexual behaviour and drugs?"

"Yes."

"The sixties and early seventies," said Vossberg. "Children from that era..." his voice trailed off. "The Summer of Love..."

"Sometimes," I said. "My legs give in when I think about it. But still, I think it is my fault."

"Yes," said Vossberg, "that's how it always plays out."

"You mean, you know other people who went through the same?"

"Not the exact circumstances, no. Besides, it is crucial that *you* recognise the patterns, not me."

"So, you think all this physical pain is mental pain from the past?"

"Absolutely. The body-mind is an extraordinary thing of complexity. It told you to stop abruptly and acknowledge the child's pain."

We both sat in the silence that followed. There was a weight on my chest, and a rock occupied the front of my skull.

"I often dream...." I began..." that there is no power in my arms. That everything slips from my hands."

"Like back then."

"Like back then."

Vossberg stood up. He slowly walked to the window, took a tin from the windowsill, opened it and presented me with a peppermint. I took it from the tin, put it on my tongue and let it melt, while Vossberg rummaged around in a desk drawer.

"Here," he said and handed me a card.

Yuki Sato, Za-Zen, it said.

"Call her," said Vossberg. I will contact her too.

Sato San's Dojo

Yuki Sato was a small bald woman who seemed to have learned by heart all she said in English. This gave her a robot-like quality.

"Zazen, arso known as "sitting meditation," is the centlal plactice of Zen Buddhism", she explained.

Like so many Japanese, she pronounced her 'r' like an 'l' and vice versa.

"We can talk in Japanese, if that's easier," I said in Japanese.

But she continued in English:

"It involves sitting in a specific posture, usually on a cushion or bench, with a straight back and an open, alert mind. The goal of zazen is to quiet the mind and become more aware of the present moment. In zazen, practitioners focus their attention on the breath, or they may use a mantra or other object of concentration to help still the mind. They may also count their breaths or use other techniques to maintain focus. The point of zazen is not to try to achieve a particular state of mind but to be aware of one's experience in the present moment without judgment or distraction. Zazen is typically done in silence, with the eyes half-closed and the mind empty and open to whatever arises. Over time, practitioners may find that they become calmer and more centred and that their awareness of the present moment deepens. Zazen is not just a meditation practice but is also a path to enlightenment or a way to awaken to one's true nature and the true nature of reality. You understand?"

"I understand."

She presented me with a square tatami mat and a flat pillow.

"*Zabuton.* Sit down, please."

She placed the pillow precisely in the middle of the tatami square.

I sat on it with my legs crossed, facing a blank wall.

She showed me how to half close my eyes and open my jaw. She looked like a crazed Butoh dancer.

I laughed and imitated her.

"Your mind is a crazy monkey," she said.

"Hes," I said through my open jaw.

"Don't talk," she said. "Just observe the crazy monkey."

My eyes rolled back, my mouth widened, and my breath deepened. The place where my head was supposed to be was one tangled mess.

"Where is your crazy monkey?" she asked.

"Ih hy head," I said.

"Wrong!" she chimed. "You have no head; you have no face. Just rook."

She was right. The mess that was supposed to be in my head was not 'in' anything. It instead was out there, with everything else.

I sneezed.

"Ahhh, nice."

Did she encourage sneezing? What madness was this?

"Aaah, coming out of the box. Nice."

I had yet to learn what she was talking about.

She led my attention to my breath. We counted my breaths in Japanese:

"*Ichi, ni, san, shi, go, roku, shichi,, hachi, kyu, ju!*"

She clapped her hands sharply.

"Wake up, wake up."

I blinked. Was this it?

"*Owari,*" she confirmed.

I got up.

The session lasted fifteen minutes or so. She stowed away the tatami mat and the zabuton. I looked around the room. There was calligraphy equipment on a table. Some scrolls with large *kanji* hung on the walls. I stepped closer to have a look.

"Ah, you like *shodo*?"

"Yes. Can you teach me?"

"Yes. I teach *shodo* too. It's about mindfulness!"

"Please," I said. "Next time."

11

Place nine: De Pinte, Belgium

Vossberg opened the session:

"Telling a child that they are feeling pleasure when they are feeling pain has a tremendously negative effect on their mental and emotional development. It leads to confusion and distrust. The child becomes less likely to trust their own feelings and perceptions and more likely to rely on external validation. Telling a child that they are not experiencing pain causes chronic pain conditions. This can lead to a cycle of pain and tension that can be difficult to break. Furthermore, minimising or denying a child's pain is emotionally damaging and can undermine their self-worth. It leads to feelings of frustration and hopelessness."

"I feel much better now, thanks!"

"Was that a joke?"

"Eh, yes. Not a very good one, I admit."

"But a little joke, nevertheless?'

"Yes, definitely a little joke."

"Progress," said Vossberg. "How was the session with Sato Sensei?"

"Rather insane."

"Yes, Zen is famous for that."

"She told me that my mind is a monkey. She will also teach me calligraphy."

"Very good. I'm pleased to hear it. Now, tell me, where are we travelling today?

"Place nine is De Pinte, a village in Belgium near Ghent. Agata's sister lived there with her husband and their five kids. It was an awful place to be. We slaved in the housekeeping and were allowed to play netball in the evenings in a field in front of the house. There were other children from the neighbourhood. It was there that I met the father of my children, Flaxen. We were thirteen. Agata had mentioned him and his brother to Flo and me as possible boyfriends."

Vossberg cleared his throat. "Right."

"You seem upset."

"A carer actively engaging in choosing potential boyfriends for a thirteen and an eleven-year-old upsets me, yes."

"They even bought us huge boxes of condoms."

"Oh boy."

"You know, I know exactly what my father would say to you now," I said.

"Do tell me."

"*I love my daughter, and she loves me. I have no idea why she is telling you all these lies. I have always looked after my girls well. You are just a little old, typically American excuse for a psychiatrist who is fucking with my daughter's mind.*"

"Thank you!"

"You're welcome."

"How do you know he would say that?"

"Because these thoughts are going through my head right now. My mind is not my own. It is his."

"Or a monkey's mind."

"Well, yes, that too."

We laughed.

"So, you got yourself a Prince. What was his name again?"

"Flaxen."

"I've never heard that name before. Did your sister hook up with his brother?"

"No, they were too young."

"And you weren't."

"Ha ha ha. That summer was beautiful, though. We did not go to Bretagne that year. Agata had ruined that anyway with her endless drills and exercises. She decided what we liked and disliked. And the worst part was, we believed her."

"However, that summer was beautiful. How?"

"A goodbye to innocence, I suppose. The first kiss, the first… you know. We spent all our time at a lake at the side of a highway in the making. We roller-skated on the new tarmac. A typical teenage holiday from a cheesy American high school movie, only I did not go to high school."

"You did not go to high school?"

"Hardly. Dad believed that school was dead. He gave me a book: *School is Dead*, by Ivan Illich."

"But he was a teacher?"

"Yes."

"So, you have no education?"

"I did my high school later, by correspondence."

"Well, that's a relief to hear. Don't tell me you were a teen bride!"

"I was."

"Pregnant too?"

"Yup!"

Vossberg and I were now talking as if this was a huge joke. And wasn't it? I began to laugh. Vossberg looked at me from the corners of his eyes. He, too, began silently shaking. We laughed until tears streamed down our cheeks.

"We are making progress, kiddo."

Sato San's Dojo

At Sato-sensei's, we engaged in a short stint of meditation. This time she compared my mind with a wild elephant. The elephant had to be tamed. The tamer was me. We put the 'pillars of breathing' around the crazy beast and tamed it by blowing air through our lips. Instead of clapping her hands to end the session, she hit me with a split bamboo bat on my shoulder from behind. This made a crazily loud noise just next to my ear. I shouted out loud with shock. She grinned. Then the Japanese calligraphy session began.

"There are three main styles of Japanese calligraphy," she said. "*Kaisho* is a formal, structured style characterised by clear, precise lines and strict adherence to the traditional forms. It is used for formal documents and certificates and is considered the standard for legibility and clarity.

Gyōsho, on the other hand, is a fluid and cursive style characterised by rounded and flowing lines. It is used for personal letters and poems.

Sōsho is a style characterised by highly fluid and exaggerated lines. It is used for artistic expression and is considered the most creative.

Each style requires a different level of skill and mastery, and each has unique aesthetic qualities. Japanese calligraphy is highly valued in Japanese culture.

We will begin with *Kaisho*."

She spread a piece of green felt on the table and placed a piece of rice paper exactly in the middle of it, just as she had done with the zabuton on the tatami mat. She placed a metal ruler along the top of the paper. A shallow stone tray was put next to my right hand. Then followed brushes in several sizes, their tips elevated by a *fude oki*. A water pitcher and an inkstone went on the tray.

Sato-sensei showed me how to move the inkstone over the tray with circular movements while breathing in and out. She added small amounts of water from the pitcher. She drew a vertical line on the paper when we had a generous puddle of pitch-black ink.

She changed the paper and gestured: Now it is your turn.

I drew a vertical line.

She placed my paper beside hers: "What is the difference?"

"Your line is straight, and mine is wobbly. Your line is sharp at the edges, and mine is frayed. Your line is beautifully shaped, like a knife, and mine looks like a sick cucumber. Your line sits on the paper in a balanced and beautiful way, and mine is all over the place."

She was beaming. "Very good!"

She sat down opposite me at the low table and began to put the calligraphy tools away methodically.

I felt strangely refreshed.

We had stared at a wall taming an imaginary monkey and elephant. Then we had drawn one vertical line, yet I felt better than I had in months.

"Rooking at the rines is vely impoltant," she said earnestly while she poured some bright orange ink into a tiny tray. She took a brush from a stand.

"Teacher's brush," she said while pointing at it.

She placed the ink-soaked tip on the paper with my stroke with an unwavering hand. She breathed in when the brush rested lightly on the paper and breathed out when she drew the line. She lifted the brush ever so elegantly and sighed deeply.

A perfect orange knife-shaped line was next to mine.

Then another one.

And another one...

"A line has three stages," she explained. "Put, pull and lift. You see: put...pull...lift."

I nodded.

"Putting things away is important too. Never wash the brushes with water."

She put the brushes between two pieces of paper and dabbed them dry, then rolled them into the green felt sheet, which was rolled into a thin bamboo mat. She folded the sheets of paper we had used to draw on and tenderly but firmly placed them into a bin.

"Garbage!"

"Are you throwing them away?"

"Yes."

"No! Give them to me?"

"No, they belong in the bin. I will make tea now. Just a moment…."

She got up, bowed and disappeared from the room. I quickly took the two folded sheets from the bin and put them in my bag.

I opened the next session with Vossberg with the following:

"This Be The Verse
By Philip Larkin

They fuck you up, your mum and dad
They may not mean to, but they do
They fill you with the faults they had
And add some extra, just for you
But they were fucked up in their turn
By fools in old-style hats and coats
Who half the time were soppy-stern
And half at one another's throats
Man hands on misery to man
It deepens like a coastal shelf
Get out as early as you can
And don't have any kids yourself."

"Gosh, I had forgotten that poem, kiddo," said Vossberg. "Were you and your half-siblings in combat?"

"Not at all. We loved the babies as soon as they were born, against our will. We had protested when they were planned, and all our fears came true; isolation and being shamed, losing more friends and family…it all came to pass. But the three adults persevered in their endeavour. They cried a lot. Despite the multiple crises… they soldiered on. Endless talk sessions were the result. We thought we talked with each other but talked to ourselves."

"The sweetness of youth."

"Sorry, why do you say that?"

"To love your half-siblings despite everything is an act of great courage."

"We had no choice."

"Right. So, from this perspective, here and now, and knowing what you know, do you still love them?"

I thought about this. Flo certainly would give the world to these kids, who were now early teens.

But did I?

"I'm not sure," I said. "They are part of my fabric now. How can I deny them."

"I'm not saying that you should. I'm trying to help you find your voice and thoughts on things."

"It has helped me greatly that you said I am a woman."

"Well, wasn't that obvious to you?"

"No."

"Well, look at you now." His aged hand moved up and down elegantly.

I looked down at my Issey Miyake dress, Comme des Garçons stockings, feminine boots… I went out of my way to be different from Dad.

"Most of all, he knows nothing about this all. Japan. You. Kunikaze… my friends…"

"Keep it that way," said Vossberg. "Distance seems the key for you."

"But Mum, I've got to talk with Mum."

"I think we're nearly ready for that if you must. Let's wait another month and see."

We. He had said *we* again. This small man in his grey pants and his grey jumper truly spoke the language of love. I told him this.

"Don't forget that you are paying me," he said, suddenly shy.

I looked at him. "Was that a joke?"

"I'm afraid so."

"But not a very good one," we said simultaneously.

"We're in zinc now," he said. "Soon, we'll be finishing each other's sentences."

"Should I tell you more?"

"You don't have to. I truly get the gist. But a bit of free-associating with the place wouldn't hurt."

"Let me think....Amersfoort....I had a great group of friends there.... Especially Elly. We're not in touch anymore. She was my neighbour. Her mum was a single parent. Mother Oak. I loved her so... I flunked out of school because school was presumably dead, while the real reason was that I had fallen too far behind. I had my first job as a draftswoman for a graphic designer... I went missing for days and lived at the horse farm. Nobody noticed... Flaxen's parents were against our relationship...."

"I wonder why," erupted Vossberg, then covered his mouth and said: "Sorry. I am so sorry!"

"It's okay. Even you make mistakes."

"I am so sorry," he said again. "Here you are trusting me, relying on me, and I come out with something so cynical."

"It's okay! Flaxen's parents were dead set against the relationship."

"Look, I *get* that. If my teenage son dated a teenage girl, I would be concerned too... but you were starved of love and needed it. So, you turned to him."

I thought about this while Vossberg brought me a peppermint. It slowly dissolved in my mouth.

I walked to my coat, a designer's dream, a Yoji Yamamoto, black and wild like a bat, and retrieved a fresh lemon from its pocket.

"This helps me when I get overwhelmed," I said. "I smell it, in shops and on the trains. Isn't that strange?"

"It is a way to be mindful of the here and now." Not strange at all." He took the lemon, smelled it and gave it back to me.

I put it back in the pocket of my coat. "Somehow, the lemon, the elephant, the monkey and the vertical line are connected," I said.

"Yes. They are. I am glad that some creativity is seeping back into you."

I laughed. I hadn't seen it that way. Vossberg often took me off guard. I laughed again. A little. Nothing big. Just two little laughs at nothing. Two little windows into a future without a mental impairment.

"How long did this *ménage à trois* last?"

"Five, six years. Years in which everything I held dear was destroyed. Our family ties were severed. We called our parents by their names and lost them that way; they became "friends" instead of parents."

"The sixties have done more harm than people think," sighed Vossberg.

"We smoked weed with them, that sort of thing. Traditional celebrations were deemed unnecessary. Gone were the birthday parties, Christmas, Easter... We were now supposed to celebrate each other and give each other presents "when we *felt* like it." Then, suddenly, my mother departed and married Said. This was the first step on the long road to recovery. Said became Lilibeth's father and, in a way, also mine. Mum shipped Flo off to Dad and Agata, who now lived in a dark brick house in Amersfoort. Mum took Lilibeth, and I moved to Leiden with Said and Mum. Said was good to me. He sent me to ballet school; he had my teeth repaired. He gave me jobs at the University of Leiden…He certainly rescued Mum from an impossible situation."

"And Flaxen?"

"His parents had held Flaxen and me apart. We both had affairs with other adult-like kids. Mine were mostly dreadful. I had a beautiful relationship with a boy named Fransje. But when Flaxen was old enough, I think sixteen, he turned up on my doorstep, and we continued what began..."

"What happened to Flo?"

"Flo, I found out later, had a terrible time at Dad's and Agata's. She was put to work as a maid by Agata. She looked after the babies. She, too, had to pay for electricity and water and labelled her own food in the fridge, like a boarder, when she was only an early teen. I only saw her occasionally. She had grown fat and grumpy. I was scared of her. But I now know that they mistreated her."

"I'm sorry to hear this. She must have been visited by trauma comparable to yours."

"Flo over-compensates by smothering her children."

"I see."

"Her trauma will manifest when the children leave the house. Mark my words."

"You are beginning to understand your predicament."

"Yes."

"With clarity comes healing, I promise you."

"I am grateful for your belief in me. What would I have done without you?'

"What would you have done?"

"Committed suicide."

"Are you still thinking about that?"

"Yes. But it seems "further away". Not so in my face anymore."

"I am so pleased to hear this. What about your vertigo?"

"Still bad. It comes in waves."

"It's very persistent."

"Alas, this is so."

12

Place ten: Leiden, the Netherlands

At Sato Sensei's tiny dojo, we tamed the 'wild elephant' and the 'crazy monkey' further by concentrating on our breath. There were, Sato explained, five types of breath. We practised them one by one. We breathed through our belly, through our chest, through our mouth and our nose. Five times each. Then we moved to what Sato called "the subtle breath". The breath through the nose softly hit the area between the nose and the upper lip. We concentrated on this area.

She hit me with the split bamboo clapper on my shoulder, and I screamed from the shock.

We moved to the calligraphy table. I now had my own calligraphy gear and set it up. I had to practice vertical strokes on one piece of paper while being aware of the stages of the stroke: put...pull....lift.

Sato did the same at the other side of the table with her bright orange ink. After I had filled five pieces of paper this way, we put them on the floor and looked at them. "Point out the good strokes."

I pointed at a couple of my strokes with the knife-like quality of Sato's work.

"It is important to *look*. Looking is as important as making."

She folded the sheets, put them in the bin and left the room to make tea. I took the rejects from the bin and put them in my bag. We drank green tea.

She had a delightful personality. Had Vossberg told her that I was sick? She told me she was so fond of tomatoes that everyone called her "Tomato-chan." Would I like her to call her that too?

"Sure, I will call you Tomato-chan," I said.

She beamed at me. Later, I would see that beaming multiplied in the monks who lived on Takai-san, a mountain west of Tokyo. These beaming faces were the key to my recovery. I decided that this was what I would like to become: a beaming face.

Vossberg began the session: "Not having access to education has a long-lasting impact on a child's development and prospects. Here are a few ways in which lack of education affects a child: Limited opportunities; Decreased cognitive development; Increased poverty; Health problems. Moreover, children who do not receive an education are more likely to suffer from health problems. Then there is social exclusion.

"Education is a fundamental human right and is critical in shaping a child's future."

"Thank you. I feel much better now. How bloody, utterly depressing!"

"Information causes healing."

"I've never seen it that way, but now I do."

"There is a doctor in New York, John Sarno, who works entirely on this principle."

"Fantastic. How lucky I am! He's in New York!"

"I am in contact with him."

"I see."

"I think you should write your mother a letter, kiddo."

"Really?"

"You're making progress. Can't you feel it?"

"If I write to Mum, I want to write to Dad too. Tell him the truth."

"That's fine with me, as long as you burn the letter to your father."

"Burn it?"

"Yes. Try it."

"Okay...."

"It is therapeutic. Discuss the letter to your mother with me before you send it, will you? Did you go to Sato Sensei this week?"

"This morning. We breathed in and out and drew vertical lines."

"That seems very minimalistic."

"It was wonderful. Exactly my cup of tea."

"Good, good. Where are you taking me today?"

"Leiden, the Netherlands. I am skipping a rather long list of boyfriends ... They were brief."

"We can come back to them later. Associating thoughts and feelings with Leiden? Isn't that a famous university city?"

"Yes, Said worked there as a researcher. He is an anthropologist. I see a big, warm, cosy house (Said's)... Mum pottering rather happily... Lilibeth going to school... Indonesian food (Said cooked it) and Indonesian things, Wajang Dolls (Said is from Java)... A canal house in a leafy street... I move in with them...Flaxen turns up....ballet, ballet, ballet... every evening of the week. I am ambitiously trying to get into a formal ballet school but fail. This is rather devastating... I finished high school, with Said's support, through a correspondence course."

"It sounds productive and balanced."

"But it didn't last long. Said and Mum went to Pakistan for Said's job."

"God, does it ever end?"

"They took Lilibeth and Flo."

"Where did you live, kiddo?"

"I stayed in their house, on the ground floor. They made me the landlord. I collected the rent. There was a Dutch couple with cats on the first floor and a Japanese couple on the second. It was a lonely period, despite Flaxen. I was pretty lost without them."

"How old were you there?"

"Sixteen, seventeen…"

"Years of abandonment."

"In a sense, yes."

"How do you mean, 'in a sense'? All your carers did was repeatedly abandon one or more of their kids."

"I've never seen it that way."

"But it's clear to me."

"Said may have asked me to come along. I don't remember…"

"The point is that you don't leave these kinds of decisions to a sixteen-year-old."

"No, maybe not."

"Not. Period. I see a kid who has never had a rest or a break. I predict that your time with Flaxen was a rollercoaster. How could it be anything else? Was it?"

"Yes."

"It is no wonder that, now that you finally found some rest, some balance, here and now, a time that you do not have to work constantly…you experience some boredom even … with Kunikaze, a decent guy in a nicely furnished flat….that you collapsed."

"Hm."

"How old are you now, kiddo?"

"Thirty."

"Have you ever been looked after like this?"

"No."

"Can you see a pattern?"

"Yes."

"But Kunikaze is not your carer."

"I know."

"Do you remember the first time you came here? The state you were in?"

"Yes."

"You said you were angry with Kunikaze for not looking after you. He is Japanese, you said, you are a foreigner in his land...He has to take the lead."

"I remember. I resented him. I still do."

"He is not your carer."

"I know."

"I'm not sure you do."

"You're right; I *know* that he is not my carer, but I *feel* he should be."

"Exactly. We have to teach your wild elephant to stand on its own feet and not crush you."

"I should not stand in my father's shoes."

"That's exactly right."

"I'm a little shit for treating Kunikaze that way."

"You are."

"Thank you."

"You are welcome."

We laughed.

13

Place eleven: Evergem, Belgium

When I went to the dojo, I called Sato-Sensei' Tomato Sensei'. This caused her to laugh uncontrollably. "You say 'Sato Sensei' *or* 'Tomato-chan', *not* "Tomato Sensei'. Ha ha ha ha ha."

Her laugh was like a bell so clear. Her session was about sound this week. The sound of the universe, she called it.

"Ohmmmmmm."

While breathing out, we said 'Ohmmmmm' twenty times. We stretched it as long as we could. It was amazing how long one sound lasted if one paid attention. The sound vibrated around the room. It was as if we were a full choir, not just the two. It was beautiful and somehow profound.

The clap on the shoulder came, I screamed, and we moved to the calligraphy table, where I was taught how to draw a horizontal line.

Put...pull...lift.

The lift was faster this time.

"Not, 'pull, pull, liiiiiift', but 'pull, pull, lift'."

"I tried it.

We compared our lines. Hers was like a bone; mine was frayed like bad knitting.

She pointed out its flaws by circling in orange where I had gone wrong.

"You lost concentration, here, here and here."

Three points where I did not pay attention in one line.

She showed me how to point my attention in one breath. She breathed in and placed the brush, she breathed out and pulled the line, and she lifted the brush...all in one moment of pure attention.

The line was perfect. Sharp-edged and slightly upwards on the page. A knife. A bone. A person almost... "Next time we cross the lines," she said, leaving the room.

I cleared the table and put our rejected drawings in my bag.

She placed the cups on the table as if they were the most precious things in the world. I began to understand why the Japanese were so good at the things they did. They concentrate on one thing at a time.

"Childhood abandonment has long-lasting effects on a person's emotional, psychological and social well-being in later life," said Vossberg. "It leads to insecurity, low self-esteem, trust issues, and difficulties in forming and maintaining relationships. It also contributes to developing mental health problems."

"Let me guess, depression and anxiety."

"Indeed."

"It was practically inescapable, this condition I have," I said.

"Yes. Did you write the letter to your mother?"

I produced the letter from the pocket of my coat. It smelled of lemon.

"Shall I read it to you?"

"Tell me first, did you write to your father too?"

"Yes, many letters. I burned them as you advised."

"How did that make you feel?"

"It made my hands go numb."

"Psychologically. How did you feel?"

"I felt very distressed. I disconnected from myself. I do not know who I am without him."

"You are in the process of finding out who you are."

"Yes."

"Read your letter, kiddo."

"Dear Mum, I am not going to call you Sjaan anymore. I want to call you Mum, as I did before Agata. Is that okay with you? Mum, would you come to visit me in Japan? I want to hang out with you a bit. We have never really done so. Like female humans, you know? I was always hijacked by Dad or by Agata. I am sorry for that. I want to talk to you about that because I have been sick. I am going to a psychiatrist three times a week. But don't worry; I am not crazy or mad. It is unclear what I am suffering from, but it has been a very tough couple of months. Kunikaze, too, would like you to come over so that you two can meet. I think you would like him. I am happy to pay if you don't have the money for a flight.

Love

Shan"

"Sounds good to me, kiddo. You might bring her here to an appointment so that we can meet and talk, perhaps."

"Don't expect too much. My mum hates to talk about serious things. She starts crying straight away."

"We will see. Where are you going to take me today? You know the drill."

"Evergem, Belgium, a small village near Ghent in Flanders. Flaxen's new home. The house was a renovated farmhouse. It was stark as a Protestant church with its whitewashed walls, marble and wooden plank floors, designer furniture and fittings...."

"How old now, kiddo?"

"Sixteen; seventeen."

"You moved to another country alone."

"Yes."

"Who was giving you money?"

"I worked for money."

"As what?"

"As a graphic designer, a drawer, a life drawing model, a cleaner…whatever I could get."

Vossberg sighed.

"I know, it's not your style," I laughed.

"My kids were still blowing out the candles on their birthday cakes each year at that age."

"Right yeah, well, Flaxen was more protected by his parents than I was. We lived with them for about a year while renovating an old house in Ghent to begin our independent lives. Flaxen's parents were, are … eh…well…mad. His father is a raging alcoholic, and his mother… oh… how to describe her… I was so scared of her. She had total control over Flaxen. Their relationship is…how can I describe it? It was as if they were negatively feeding off each other."

"Co-dependent?"

"I don't know what that means."

"A co-dependent relationship between a mother and son is characterised by an unhealthy emotional dependence on one another. In this dynamic, the mother relies on her son for emotional fulfilment and validation, while the son looks to his mother for approval, guidance, and support in all areas of his life. This type of relationship limits the son's ability to develop healthy relationships and boundaries. On the other hand, the mother struggles to let go of her emotional dependence on her son and has difficulty setting healthy boundaries for their relationship. The son feels pressured to prioritise his mother's needs over his own, leading to resentment and frustration. The mother becomes overly involved in her son's life and tries to control his decisions and choices, which can cause him to feel suffocated and restricted.."

I blew air through my lips.

"Pfff, that is exactly how it is. Flaxen's mother did not like me and tried to convince Flaxen to break up with me. When I fell pregnant, she tried to force me to abort the child."

"Still, you lived with her for a year?"

"Yes. I must say, we were not the best kids to have around either. We wrecked the house. We were renovating and walked dirt everywhere. The bathtub became so damaged that they had to install a new one. The wood plank floor had to be revarnished…The house was their pride. We should have been more considerate."

"What about the dad?"

"He frequently passed out from alcohol. Still, I liked him somehow. Like my dad, he is an artist, a painter, but he was a caricature… He was like people imagine an artist to be: unreasonable, passionate and drunk. He was famous too. They had money. He did not seem to mind me. I had crazy conversations with him on the staircase at four in the morning. He was already drinking his first lemonade glass full of liquor at that hour…."

"This must have all had quite an effect on Flaxen, I imagine."

"I am only beginning to understand this now. Flaxen is a very inhibited person. He trembles when touched, like a rabbit. He does everything his mother says, albeit while protesting."

"Was he ever sexually abused by his mother?"

This startled me. I fell silent. Something in me shifted toward understanding. I thought about it. Vossberg brought me a peppermint. It dissolved in my mouth slowly. Had Flaxen experienced something similar to me? Or worse? Somehow, it seemed entirely possible. Plausible even. Did Flaxen live with the same poison pumping through his veins as I had? Was this why we connected on the deep level we once thought we did? Was this why there had been a recognition between us? I voiced these thoughts to Vossberg slowly and uneasily. "But I don't know for sure," I concluded. "He never told me anything of that nature. But then, he did not talk easily, except after ten glasses of beer. It is too late to ask now. He is married to another woman now. You do know, Doctor Vossberg, how to cut to the chase."

"That's my job."

"You're good at it."

"Thanks, kiddo."

At Tomato-chan's, I had to imagine myself to be a mountain while I sat on the zazen mat. This was surprisingly easy and comforting. My body felt like a rock. At the top, where my head was, was a mess of monkeys and elephants fighting. I told Tomato-chan this after she landed the clapper on my shoulder, and I screamed.

"You have no head," she said. "No face either. Your face is everywhere. See? In the mirror, the TV screen, the spoon, in me, because I see you… except where it is supposed to be."

Somehow, this rang true.

"Is that a koan?" I asked.

Tomato-chan laughed her bell-like laugh. "No, a koan is different. A koan is a story. A story to startle your elephant."

At the calligraphy table, we crossed the horizontal and the vertical line, at one-third of the lengths of the lines. We drew lopsided crosses until the ink ran out.

Put, pull, lift slow, Put, pull, lift a little faster. Dip and start anew.

Tomato-chan corrected my strokes with her orange ink.

We put the sheets of paper on the ground, and I pointed out the best one.

"That one you can take home."

"Thank you."

She left the room. I took the rejects from the bin and put them in my bag. We sipped our tea while talking about swimming. Tomato-chan loved to swim. She was good at the butterfly stroke. She was utterly void of irony or sarcasm. She resembled a child, serious and disarming, chatting about this and that with full attention. How old would she be? It was hard to tell.

Tofuya Ukai, Tokyo Tower

I was so sick of having vertigo that I decided to confront it head-on. I would *seek* vertigo instead of running away from it. Why had I not thought of that before? From Min Tanaka, I learned long ago that if one breathes and goes toward the pain with one's mind, the pain disappears or lessens.

"I want to visit high places in Tokyo," I told Kunikaze. "Places that make you sick with vertigo."

"Tokyo Tower," he said. Let's go on Saturday."

Standing three-hundred-thirty-three metres high in the centre, Tokyo Tower was the world's tallest, self-supported steel tower. Typical of the economic boom, it was three metres taller than its model, the Eiffel Tower. It symbolised Japan's post-war rebirth as a major economic power. It was the highest building in Tokyo. In addition to being a tourist spot, it served as a broadcast antenna.

First, we went to the main deck at hundred and fifty metres, by elevator. There were lookdown windows in the floor. You could stand on them. This served my purpose. I stood on one of the windows, looking down and concentrating on the vertigo lashing my body. I realised that physical and mental vertigo are the same.

A second set of elevators connected the main deck to the 250-metre-high top deck, from where one can get a bird's eye view of Tokyo, high above the surrounding buildings. Visibility was good; we could see Mount Fuji in the distance. There too, I exposed myself as much as I could to the feeling of vertigo.

Afterwards, in the building at the base of the tower, known as Foot Town, we went to a restaurant that featured pine trees and a pond with *Koi*. It was an unlikely oasis tucked away from the hustle and bustle of the city. Passing the garden lantern and waterwheel and walking on the stepping stone, we found ourselves in Edo, the Tokyo of 200 years ago. It was surreal.

The restaurant was inside a two-hundred-year-old sake brewery, transported to the tower from Yonezawa, Yamagata Prefecture, within a samurai-era merchant's residence.

As we were greeted by the kimono-clad staff and escorted to our private dining room via the winding passages and silent hallways, we looked at the traditional elements of the Japanese interior: massive polished beams, sunken hearth, ancient vats and a wooden sake press.

The room was furnished in traditional *zashiki*-style: tatami mats, form screens and windows backed with translucent paper. Everything exuded a simple and timeless Japanese aesthetic. The floor-to-ceiling windows allowed views of the meticulously manicured Japanese garden where a waterwheel turned. A few Momiji trees were still in bloom.

The menu revolved around tofu, incorporated into *kaiseki*, full courses of traditional Japanese cuisine. The tofu was produced at their workshop in the Okutama mountains behind Hachioji from beans grown in Hokkaido. Made and delivered daily, the tofu was the best we'd ever tasted.

We ordered the nine-course lunch *Matsu* set. It was elaborate, featuring a ceramic *nabe* hot pot of homemade rich and velvety tofu in seasoned soy milk, quail dumpling and taro cake, strips of deep-fried *abura-age* grilled over charcoal and basted with a special sweet-savoury miso sauce, fresh sashimi, simmered tofu dumpling with crab, and deep-fried blowfish.

We ended our set with sweet potato on rice, miso soup and pickles, fragrant *shincha* green tea; and, as dessert, a toasted sesame tofu with black sesame red bean paste.

The service was impeccable, and we were allowed to linger as long as we liked in our room. Tearing ourselves away from this tranquil, pampering oasis, where everything was balanced, was hard.

14

Place twelve: Ghent, Belgium

At the beginning of the session, Vossberg said: "Sexual assault, no matter who the perpetrator is, has severe and long-lasting effects on the victim. When a boy is sexually assaulted by his mother, it can be especially traumatic and confusing, as the person responsible for protecting and caring for him has betrayed that trust. The boy experiences fear, shame, guilt, anger, and depression. He struggles with trust and may have difficulty forming healthy relationships. He has difficulty with intimacy and sexuality and struggles with substance abuse or self-harm. Healing is possible, and many survivors of sexual assault live fulfilling lives. However, the road to recovery is long and difficult."

"Flaxen certainly struggled with trust. He once was convinced that I had slept with his friend while I had not. He was unreliable. He had affairs. He drinks a lot. He would never go to a therapist. I feel sorry for his current wife. I had the best part of him: the very young and beautiful, idealistic Flaxen."

"There is a hereditary component to the development of alcoholism. The risk of developing alcoholism is between forty and sixty per cent higher. Genetics is just one factor that contributes to the development of alcoholism. Other factors, such as peer pressure, stress, and mental health conditions, also play a role."

"We were both rather unlucky then, Flaxen and I, don't you think?"

"I suppose you could say that. You both came from dysfunctional families and had no information about what could help you move on."

"That's exactly right. Both families did not believe in therapy. And is an alcoholic not automatically a narcissist?"

"No, the two conditions are separate and distinct. Alcoholism is a progressive and chronic disease. Narcissistic personality disorder is a mental health condition characterised by a lack of empathy for others."

"What about a parent who sexually abuses a child? Are they not automatically narcissists?"

"While some who engage in child sexual abuse may exhibit narcissistic traits, not all individuals who sexually abuse children are necessarily diagnosed with a narcissistic personality disorder. Child sexual abuse can be motivated by various factors, including a desire for power and control, mental illness or trauma, and a distorted or deviant sexual preference. The abuser does not fully understand the impact of their behaviour and is acting out of a distorted sense of affection or desire for closeness. Those who engage in child sexual abuse can come from all walks of life and may not exhibit obvious warning signs or behavioural patterns."

"There was a deep sense of recognition between Flaxen and me. Do you think victims of sexual abuse unconsciously recognise each other?"

"There is limited research on that; as far as I know, I suppose it is possible. Trauma affects a person's social interactions and how they relate to others. Those who have experienced similar types of trauma may have similar patterns of behaviour and ways of relating to others. Victims of sexual abuse may not disclose their experiences, and some may not even be aware of the extent of their experiences' impact on their lives. Not all victims of sexual abuse respond to their experiences in the same way."

"I see."

"I assume the next place you are taking me is the ground where it all played out?"

"Yes, Ghent, Belgium. It took us a year to renovate the new house, a ruin from the eleventh century."

"Amazing."

"Flaxen's brother, Sebastiaan, was involved in the renovation too. He moved in with us. My two boys were born in that house and spent the first years of their lives there."

"It does not cease to amaze me how resilient you were, Shan. Renovate a whole house! Was there anything you couldn't do?"

I fell silent.

Vossberg went to fetch a peppermint from the windowsill.

"You don't take compliments well. How come?"

"You tell me."

"How does a compliment make you feel?"

I closed my eyes while thinking about it. "I feel disbelief. I feel like an imposter."

"There may be several reasons for this. You may have low self-esteem or a negative self-image and may not believe you deserve praise or recognition. In that case, accepting a compliment can feel threatening or uncomfortable. You are sensitive to perceived criticism or negativity, even in the form of a compliment. For you, compliments may trigger anxiety or insecurity, and you may not know how to respond. You may also feel you do not want to seem arrogant or egotistical. You may feel that acknowledging your strengths or accomplishments is inappropriate or will lead to unwanted attention or criticism. Accepting compliments is a skill that can be learned and improved."

"I see."

"With that out of the way, tell me, in associating words, the experience of Ghent, Belgium."

"Poverty. Dust. Exhaustion. Love."

"Did Flaxen not work?"

"In the beginning, he was still studying. He flunked all his exams and never got his degree. Then he got a job as an apprentice with an architect who underpaid him, arguing that most architecture apprentices with degrees were not paid at all. I worked, did the housekeeping and looked after the children. The renovation was never finished. Hence the dust. There was love, for sure, but resentment was slipping in too. I was envious of those with working husbands who lived in dust-free houses."

"What kind of work did you do?"

"I had a dance company, and I worked for a theatre company, *Creeping Poverty*. It was the early eighties. There was an economic downturn. Work was scarce. I cleaned rooms in an orphanage. It was all very very difficult. Until we moved to Japan, that changed everything."

"Flaxen and the children came with you?"

"They came later when I had established a base. I had a job, a big flat...."

"It seems you were doing all the heavy lifting in this relationship."

"That's exactly right. It's the same in his current marriage. She has two jobs. Flaxen is doing quite well now with his furniture design, but he never got over not becoming a real architect. His mother blames me for that, of course... and Flaxen drinks like a fish, far worse than before."

"He is in Belgium, right?"

"Yes."

"So how do you know all this stuff, and how did he return to Belgium?"

"I go four to six times a year to Europe. Flaxen's mother came to fetch him and the children. He said to me he would be back with the children. He just had to satisfy his mother. I begged him not to go. I said we could live anywhere he wanted but not near his mother... We'll be back, he said. Don't worry, he said. The next thing I knew, he was married to someone else."

"But you were married to him. There must have been a divorce?"

"No. They annulled the marriage somehow. I, to this day, do not know how."

"God almighty," said Vossberg. "So why Japan? How did you end up choosing Japan? It's not the most obvious destination."

"I did a course here with Min Tanaka."

"I see."

"You know Min Tanaka?"

"Yes, I've seen his performances."

"Really?!"

I could not put Vossberg and Min Tanaka together. How was this rather conservative American interested in the naked dancer?

"I'm perhaps not the conservative American you take me for."

"A mind reader you are."

"I find his performances quite interesting."

"I got a grant from the Belgian government twice to study with him."

"Are you still with him?"

"No. Two reasons: chronic back pain and the group may become a cult."

"I've heard that too."

"How have you heard this?"

"I can't say. Confidentiality…."

"I see."

I thought of the few foreigners in the dance group. One of them must be seeing or has seen Vossberg too. Whom would that be? I was still in touch with most of them. But then, my American friend Arturo knew Vossberg and had put me in touch with him. Arturo knew the foreign Maijuku members… the expat community in Tokyo was rather small…

"It's a small world," said Vossberg.

"You're reading my mind again."

"Any news from your mother, kiddo?"

"Not yet."

Tomato-chan's Dojo

At Tomato-chan's dojo, I had to imagine that I was a valley with a lake. The wind blows over the lake and takes all my thoughts and feelings. It was effortless. I became utterly empty. It was most refreshing. My breath joined the wind and stopped. I was motionless, and time stopped. It was a bit like a spell. Clap. I screamed. Tomato-chan beamed.

I put away the tatami mat and the zabuton.

"I am very proud of you," she said.

"Why? I did nothing."

"Exactly," she said.

We moved to the calligraphy table, where we practised drawing diagonal lines. I put them all over the paper, overlapping each other.

"Good!" she said.

She was practising in a more controlled manner with her orange ink. Her strokes were like rain.

We put them next to each other on the ground and pointed out the best ones. We always agreed on the best ones. She said that was normal. "Everybody can see the best one, even children."

"Why would that be?"

"It's nature; nature's harmony. *Wa*. Everybody likes *wa*."

Wa

Wa is a cultural concept meaning "harmony". It implies a peaceful unity and conformity within a social group in which members prefer community over their interests.

Wa is considered integral to Japanese society and derives from traditional family values.

People who break the ideal of *wa* to further their purposes are brought in line by reprimands from a superior or by their family or colleagues' tacit disapproval. Hierarchical structures primarily exist for the continuation of *wa*. Disagreement is suppressed in the interest of preserving communal harmony.

Kunikaze's businesses encouraged *wa* in the workplace. Employees were given a career for life to foster a strong association with their colleagues and the company. Rewards and bonuses were given to groups rather than individuals.

Wa could be found everywhere, in architecture or how a meal was arranged on a plate.

Kunikaze's conflict avoidance was based on *wa*. He *did* have dissenting thoughts and got frustrated. It was just that achieving *wa* was crucial to his social values; he distinguished between *honne*, his true feelings, and *tatemae*, the face he wore in public. While Western culture may view this as hypocrisy, he understood that rising above his personal feelings for the good of society had its virtue – he was not a hypocrite but a good citizen.

I admired this quality in the Japanese. Then why did I get so irritated by Kunikaze?

Why the perception gap? I went to Kinokuniya and bought books about *wa*.

It learned about Japan's agricultural history and how it shaped a culture that values harmony. Its geographic isolation, mountainous terrain and few natural resources necessitated cooperation between farmers, who relied upon one another to maintain the irrigation systems required to grow rice and other crops. To survive and thrive, farmers had to work together and place the needs of their farming communities above their own to remain productive. *Wa* was necessary for survival.

This concept was formalised for all Japanese society in A.D. 604 when Prince Shōtoku decreed in Japan's first constitution: "*Wa* should be valued and quarrels avoided. When superiors are in harmony with each other, and inferiors are friendly, affairs are discussed quietly, and the right view of matters prevails.

For Westerners, for who speaking one's mind and tackling differences head-on is seen as being faithful to one's self, the concept of *wa* may seem antiquated.

When I understood why Kunikaze valued harmony, I could begin to appreciate that it was more than simply being polite, patient or agreeable. It was a result of actions, words, and gestures. It was the sum of millions of people with a shared value that guides them daily. At a time when Western culture was pulling people apart, *wa* bound people together.

15

The Turning Point

"How are your symptoms, kiddo?" asked Vossberg.

"I barely dare to say it aloud, but I think they are getting slightly weaker."

I told Vossberg about fighting vertigo with vertigo in high places.

"That's terrific news."

"My mother is arriving in a month."

"Kiddo! We're making progress."

"All thanks to you."

Vossberg was silent. He seemed to shrink away in his armchair. "You are making it happen, kiddo, not me."

"That's not true. You saved my life."

"Nah," said Vossberg softly.

"Do I detect an inability to take a compliment?"

"Smartass."

He walked to the window and took a peppermint. He stared out of the window absent-mindedly.

"Can I have a peppermint too?"

"Oh, sorry," he said, still not wholly present.

"What are you thinking about?"

"That, in your case, information brings healing. It is quite extraordinary. It makes me think of a diagnosis, but I must do more research first."

"You mean, what I have has a name after all?"

"Maybe. Watch this space. I am going to consult Dr Sarno in New York."

"Should I be worried?"

"No, please, no. Take me to your next destination instead..."

I want to stay where we were for a bit; I mean, what is happening in real-time, here in Tokyo and in Ghent, where my children are."

"Okay, go ahead."

"This is very difficult. I get dizzy just thinking about it. I see lights flashing and feel vertigo all through my body."

"Take your time, kiddo; you've done it before; you can do it again. The only way is through it, remember?"

I breathed in deeply, held my breath and exhaled noisily. I was on the verge of tears immediately.

"Something very strange is happening to Flaxen. He is getting famous. He has one breakthrough after another lately."

"That seems a good thing?"

"Well, no, not really. He is taking it badly. He is into drugs and models."

"I thought he was married?"

"That has never stopped him..."

"I see."

"His wife is pregnant with their second. He's never sober. His work has made a huge jump toward professionalism... he is producing the floating furniture he once described to me when we were children... It's made with extraordinary precision and innovation... you have to X-ray it to know how it works. So, there are two simultaneous opposite developments: the more perfect his furniture becomes, the more his private life unravels. His furniture is about to leave private production and go into mass production. He is on TV a lot...He is drunk as a skunk during most interviews. He flirts with every female reporter who interviews him and slurs his words. It is most embarrassing, especially for the children."

"He is following in his father's footsteps."

"Unbelievably so, yes. The last time I saw him, about five months ago, he looked exactly like his father. He had aged immensely. I hardly recognised him. His face was red and swollen…He was cruel to his wife."

"Abusive?"

"Borderline. Just very unpleasant."

"Is it time to get the children to Japan?"

I thought about this. We were silent for a long time.

"No," I said.

"Why not?"

"Because they are not, as his wife correctly pointed out, a pair of suitcases."

"You agree with his wife?"

"Yes."

"You like her?"

"Not really, but I respect her."

"She is raising your children."

"Yes."

"And you're okay with that."

"Yes."

"Why?"

"Because I have let them go. They have let me go. The pain of that was, *is*, nearly unbearable. We would tear all these wounds open again if we moved them. Besides, they are like their father; they are born designers. They will follow in *his* footsteps, not mine. They are made with his genetic material. They are already building things. They need to be where they are to develop these skills further. In the family business, which is finally taking off."

I was crying.

Vossberg handed me a box of tissues.

"This is my greatest pain. It will never cease, go away, or stop, except in death. All I can do is bear it."

Vossberg handed me a peppermint.

"Oh kiddo," he said, "Oh kiddo, kiddo."

I walked to the window. It was a grey rainy day. Outside, traffic spattered mud onto the sidewalk. Pedestrians with umbrellas hurried past. I was aware how grief coursed within my blood through my body, filling my chest with pain, my head with pressure, my lips with numbness, my throat with thumping contractions, down to my belly where it caused the havoc of a stampeding herd, around to my lower back and hips, down my legs into my numb feet.

I limped back to my chair. "It's grief that is destroying me."

"Yes," said Vossberg almost inaudibly.

We sat silently for a long time in the face of these inescapable facts.

"Flaxen said he'd come back," I whispered.

Vossberg nodded quietly.

"But he didn't. I am escaping a tragedy. The tragedy of his demise."

When I finally stood up, Vossberg walked me to the door as if I were an invalid. I leaned heavily on his arm. He let me go like he released a bird back into the wild, or a butterfly. Outside, a gale was blowing. My umbrella broke, and I got soaked. I cancelled my session with Tomato-chan. Kunikaze was on a business trip to Osaka. I was home alone.

The Spirit of the Fox attacks

I took off my shoes at the *genkan,* my coat, my dress, and my underwear... while walking to the tatami room behind the living room. Leaving a trail of wet clothes, I lay down naked on the cool mats. They smelled of green tea. I stared at the ceiling through my tears. It was made of smooth wood. Or was it plastic? I could hear the gale raging around our apartment block. I closed my eyes and, for the first time, allowed myself to feel the pain. I had been betrayed twice, first by my father and then by my husband. I had never thought of it that way. But there it was. Crisp and clear.

My naked body was like a landscape. There were mountains, and there were valleys. The pain was like a herd of cattle causing havoc in it. The herd stampeded blindly; it meandered through every nook and cranny. It was leaving a broad trail of destruction. This was the Spirit of the Fox. I had come to its source. I surrendered to the stampeding herd. The landscape trembled, shook and thundered. I was sure I was going to be trampled. I rolled around under the furious hoofbeats while protecting my head with my arms.

I must have passed out.

When I woke up, the sun was shining. Kunikaze was taking off his shoes at the door. His entering the front door must have woken me. He followed the track of clothes, picking them up from the floor. He sat beside me and put a cool hand on my forehead. We looked at each other. There was despair in his eyes.

I nodded at him and said: "It will be okay; I'll be okay."

He fetched a duvet from the cupboard and covered me. I drifted away. In my half-dream, I could see a group of workmen in a valley at the end of a tunnel through a mountain. They were sticking their spades in the earth, wiping the sweat off their foreheads and the dirt off their hands.

I sat up and imagined my body was a valley with a lake. The wind blew over the lake and took all my thoughts and feelings. It was effortless. I became empty. It was refreshing. My breath joined the wind and stopped. I was completely motionless, and time seemed to stop too. It was a bit like a spell. The door opened, and the wind must have caught it. Kunikaze came in. I screamed.

I told Kunikaze about Tomato-chan.

"She calls herself a nun in the wild."

"How long have you been going there?"

"About six months."

"And you are telling me only now? Why?"

"Because, Kinikaze, I don't want to talk about me all the time. I want to live in *wa*."

"Only Japanese can do *wa*."

"See, this is exactly what I mean. You keep separating us in Japanese and *gaijin*."

"But that is what we *are*."

I could not argue with that. I threw my hands in the air. "You win."

16

The diagnosis

"I think I have a diagnosis," said Vossberg.
"I have one, too," I said.
"You do?"
"A broken heart."
I told him about the stampeding herd.
"You are right. But a broken heart is not considered a psychiatric condition. However, the intense emotional pain and distress accompanying a broken heart can certainly have psychological and behavioural effects and may lead to psychiatric disorders.
"Let me guess: such as depression, anxiety, or post-traumatic stress disorder."
"That's right."
"I'm nearly a psychiatrist, like you."
He laughed.
"There is something called Broken Heart Syndrome, also called stress-induced cardiomyopathy or *takotsubo*."
"*Takotsubo* is an octopus trap."
"That's right. The traps resemble the shape of a heart."
Women are more likely than men to experience sudden, intense chest pain — the reaction to a surge of stress hormones — that an emotionally stressful event can cause.

Broken heart syndrome is often misdiagnosed as a heart attack because the symptoms and test results are similar. Dramatic changes in rhythm and blood substances are typical of a heart attack. But unlike a heart attack, there's no evidence of blocked heart arteries. In broken heart syndrome, a part of your heart temporarily enlarges and doesn't pump well while the rest of your heart functions normally. It can lead to severe, short-term heart muscle failure. It is treatable. Most people who experience it fully recover within weeks. The most common symptoms are chest pain, shortness of breath, and cardiogenic shock. Some symptoms differ from those of a heart attack. The EKG, a test that records the heart's electrical activity, the results don't look the same as the EKG results for a person having a heart attack. Tests show no signs of heart damage or blockages in the coronary arteries. They show ballooning and unusual movement of the lower left heart chamber. Your test results did not indicate Broken Heart Syndrome."

"What is it then?"

"It is called TMS—Tension Myoneural Syndrome. I have spoken about you to my colleague in New York City, Dr John Sarno, a physician and professor of rehabilitation medicine who developed a theory that posits that many cases of chronic pain, particularly back pain, neck pain, and headache, are caused not by structural problems in the body but by psychological factors, particularly unconscious emotional conflicts and stress. According to John's theory, the mind produces tension in response to psychological stress, which can manifest as physical symptoms such as pain, tingling, numbness, and weakness. Sarno believes the unconscious mind creates this tension to distract the person from emotional issues they find difficult to confront. The physical symptoms of TMS, in other words, serve as a smokescreen that allows people to avoid dealing with psychological stress and emotional conflicts.

John's approach to treating TMS involves educating and informing patients about the psychological origins of their symptoms and encouraging them to take an active role in managing their pain. While the theory of TMS is controversial, it is still influential, and many patients have reported significant improvement in their symptoms following treatment.

"I have been unable to prescribe medication, although I have wanted to several times. Yet, you have responded well to my treatment, which consisted mainly of providing you with information. This indicates to me that you have TMS.

"Your brain is sending pain signals to your body mistakenly. This is why no abnormalities show in scans and other medical tests.

It means that we have been doing it right from the get-go and that it was a blessing in disguise that I could not prescribe you any medication."

"While you were doing your research with Doctor Sarno, I lay naked on the tatami floor for days while I faced a herd of cattle that stampeded through me. I have seen, in half-sleep, a group of workmen who stuck their spades in the earth and wiped their brows as if a huge job was done."

"How extraordinary."

"I have talked with Kunikaze, and after Mum has been here, we will go to Belgium to see the children."

"Excellent.

"I have brought you a book by John Sarno. It is about back pain and its causes and the treatment of TMS. I want you to broaden the scope to all symptoms you have while reading it because it is my professional opinion that TMS can cause all the symptoms you have been suffering from."

I took the book from his hands: *Mind Over Back Pain*.

"Thank you."

"I think we can reduce your visits to twice a week now."

"You're weaning me off?"

"Yes. Just a little."

At Tomato-chan's, we concentrated on the subtle breath. She kept calling it the 'subtre bleth' although I had tried to correct her many times.

The spot where the breath from the nose hits the face differs for everyone. For Tomato-chan, it was between the lips and the nose; for me, it was on the right side of my upper lip.

With my eyes half closed and my mouth hanging half open, I pinpointed my attention to that little point on my body while facing a blank wall.

The subtle point seemed to expand.

It engulfed me.

I became the point.

The clap on the shoulder came out of nowhere. A minute could have gone by or a day. I screamed. Tomato-chan beamed. "You are very good at this!"

"I do nothing at all."

"Exactly!"

We moved to the calligraphy table and practised the counterpart to the diagonal line we had drawn the week before. Last week's line was from left to right with a long 'lift' part.

This week's line was from right to left and had a *stop* at the end.

Put, draw, stop, lift.

Put, draw, stop, lift.

We put the sheets of paper on the floor and looked.

We chose the best ones.

Tomato-chan left the room.

I stole the drawings that were meant for the bin.

We drank tea.

Tomato-chan beamed.

Her head gleamed in the lamplight.

I opened John E. Sarno's book *Mind Over Back Pain* and started reading it. I found myself on every page. I had TMS. The Spirit of the Fox had a name, after all.

"Losing custody of one's children in a divorce can have significant psychological consequences for the mother," began Vossberg. "Some potential psychological consequences are..."

"Let me guess. Depression and anxiety."

"She feels sad, hopeless, and guilty and experiences symptoms such as difficulty sleeping, loss of appetite, and lack of energy. If the mother believes that the custody decision was unfair or unjust, she may feel anger and resentment. Self-doubt and questioning one's abilities follow. Then, social isolation. The mother may wonder if she did something wrong or is not good enough to care for her children. The mother may feel like a failure. She may feel ashamed to socialise with others with children.

"Well, all of the above: tick, tick, tick" I said, "except social isolation. I am the champion of friendships."

"Have you read Sarno's book?"

"I did. I found myself on every page. I did all the tests. I have TMS. I have begun reacting to my symptoms differently."

"How?"

"It's a bit embarrassing."

"Oh."

"But I'll tell you anyway."

"Good."

"When a wave of pain arrives, I speak to my brain. I say: 'Brain, my spine is fine. You are sending the wrong signals to it. Please stop it. Now!' I repeat this several times. This makes the pain waver. I am not kidding. It makes an immediate difference to the pain. If the pain does persist, I close my eyes and engage in eh... prayer. I do not believe in God, but still, I pray. I speak to my dead ancestors. I ask them to gather 'in the light of God'. I don't know why I say that, but I do. I wait until they gather in my mind's eye. Opa van R, Oma V and Uncle Arne, my uncle who electricuted himself, Maaike's father... anybody I know who is dead...and I ask them to help me get better and understand my pain. I ask them to work together.

I stretch out my arms to them.
I hold my Oma's hand in the air..."
"And you find this embarrassing?"
"Yes, very."
"I think it is moving and very very cool."
"Really?'
Vossberg blinked away a tear.
"Yes, kiddo."

Shame

I felt at home in Japan because I recognised its culture of shame.

It was Ruth Benedict who first called Japan a "shame society." She writes:

A society that inculcates absolute standards of morality and relies on men's developing a conscience is a guilt culture by definition.... In a culture where shame is a major sanction, people are chagrined about acts which we expect people to feel guilty about. This chagrin can be very intense and it cannot be relieved, as guilt can be, by confession and atonement.... Where shame is the major sanction, a man does not experience relief when he makes his fault public even to a confessor.

True shame cultures rely on external sanctions for good behavior, not, as true guilt cultures do, on an internalized conviction of sin. Shame is a reaction to other people's criticism...

If you do this, if you do that," their elders say, "the world will laugh at you.

I began to learn that the rules in Japan revolved around etiquette. The rules required subordinating oneself to the duties to neighbours, family and country.

Benedict saw the fear of ridicule and ostracism beginning early in life. She understood how a failure to follow the expected good behaviour was *haji*.

I read Chie Nakane, professor of social anthropology at the Institute of Oriental Culture. She showed the importance of the group and its role within Japanese society.

She talked about *frame* and *attribute*. Frame puts people into a group. *Attribute* means being a member of a group.

In group identification, a frame such as a 'company' or 'association' is of primary importance; the attribute of the individual is a secondary matter.

Once an individual enters a group, their relationship with others remains the same for the duration of that relationship, whether in a family, school or business.

Japanese finds their world clearly divided into three categories, sempai (seniors), kohai (juniors) and doryo (same rank).

In order to be accepted and effective in a group, an individual needs to go along with the decisions of the group. If one opposes the group's decision, he/she will be opposed. "Indeed, it often happens that once a man has been labelled as one whose opinions run contrary to those of the group, he will find himself opposed on any issue and ruled out by majority opinion. No one will defend him in any circumstances.

Control helps to regulate in-group behavior, but it limits the expression of thoughts and ideas.

The feeling that 'I must do this because A and B also do it or they will laugh at me unless I do such-and-such' rules the life of the individual with greater force than any other consideration and thus has a deep effect on decision-making.

With group consciousness so highly developed, there is almost no social life outside the particular group on which an individual's major economic life depends. The individual's every problem must be solved within the frame."

The behaviour of one individual affects the group. If one person does something embarrassing it reflects on the groups they are a member of.

This strong emphasis on *wa* has a secondary effect: shame.

Being laughed at is felt to be unpleasant; in Japan, it is the most drastic sanction of all, more dreaded by most than the most incredible physical pain and deprivation. The unpleasant feeling of fearing mockery, of bashfulness, is called *hazukashii* .

Not losing face is a significant motivator in Japan. A unique psychopathology from conflict is *shinkeishitsu*, an unconscious fear that *wa* is disturbed.

Another area that has been linked to shame is dependency or *amae*. It is the noun form of *amaeru*, which means "to depend upon another's benevolence. This word has the same root as *amai*, an adjective that means "sweet." *Amaeru* is used to describe a child's attitude toward their parents. It affirms dependency, a psychological attempt to deny separation from the mother.

For Westerners, dependency is okay in infancy but is seen as unhealthy in later life. But this concept is alive and well in Japan. The person's *toraware* (to be bound or caught) quickly turns into hypersensitivity in his relationship with others. This hypersensitivity is described by the word *kodawari*. It is the noun form of *kodawaru*, which means "to be sensitive to minor things," or "to be inwardly disturbed over one's relationships." In the state of *kodawari* one feels that one is not accepted by others, which suggests that *kodawari* results from the unsatisfied desire to *amaeru*.

Japanese have no sense of self, apart from their desire to *amaeru*. "No-self." is an essential concept in Buddhism.

The tendency to be the recipient of love only produces gratitude; and gratitude leads to shame.

This understanding of self, or no-self, differs from the Westerner. Japanese therapists have referred to their clients as onions: When you peel all the layers off, you get down to nothing. Patients are brought up to be closely in touch with others' feelings, needs, and moods while entirely out of touch with their own. When asked what they are feeling usually elicits no response.

Shaming is the result of and the cause of no-self.

I thought about when Vossberg asked me what I liked about myself, and I answered: my shoes. I thought about the net of shame that had fallen over me at a young age. I had more in common with the Japanese than Kunikaze thought. But I could not explain it to him.

17

The aftermath

The Spirit of the Fox raged relentlessly for a year and a half. Then, I had vivid visions of workmen cleaning their hands and sticking their spades in the dirt at the end of a tunnel that led through a mountain. I was amazed by the cheesy nature of the image. The cliché of it!

My visits to Dr Vossberg were reduced to twice a week and then to once.

This did not mean all symptoms were gone. The hot pan in my head was still there, and so were the numb and tingling hands. My feet had joined in too. It was as if my limbs were filled with popping candy. The strong urge to apologise to Mum remained. I had not looked after her enough as a child, I felt.

Mum came, and Mum went.

She let me apologise and take her on a trip around Japan.

I thought this would help her and me heal.

I took her to Kyoto and Nara. We fed the deer in the streets of Nara and ate shaved ice on the Philosopher's Path in Kyoto. We bathed in *onsen*, stayed in *ryokan*, and walked in the mountains in Daigo, where we visited the local wooden Shinto shrine and the rock I had spent the night years ago during the Maijuku intensive.

"Why would you do such a thing?" Mum wondered.

When I wanted to talk about the past, she said that Dad was a devil and that it was no wonder I had gone bonkers.

"We never did anything girl-like, you and me," I said. "Why?"
She did not answer.
I tried to make up for what we had missed by buying her lipsticks in different colours and by writing her messages on the mirrors of our hotel room's bathrooms:

Good morning, Mum, I love you.

Hi Mum!

Mum! Let's have a good day!

She did not acknowledge the messages.
She wrote home that I was wearing only silken underwear; I heard later from Flo.
It was not true. I don't know where she got that bit. Why did Mum lie about underwear? Why was she like this?

Mum gossiped about Flo. Flo, she said, was mad and spent too much money.
I did not get caught in the triangle-ing this time.
Triangle-ing was what my family did.
I did not take the bait. I had learned. This fact changed Mum's behaviour somewhat. She stopped gossiping.
When she left, I felt we were a tiny bit closer. But not so close that I could tell her about Dad and the snake poison.
The silken underwear incident, I thought, was similar to what had happened on that birthday when Mum grabbed the pink baby doll, held it against her body and said: "Look, this is what Dad gave me! Isn't it pretty?" While Dad had given her a camera.
She had wide blue eyes when she said it, open and honest.
Even I knew, at that tender age, that Dad had given her the camera.
Why did Mum do such things?

Why was she like this?

We visited temples and shrines and ate Japanese food.
Mum received easily as if the world owed her. She didn't give easily. She had, I realised, nothing to give.
She was happy when I told her Kunikaze and I would go and see the children. She liked Kunikaze.

Mum came and went, and it was as if a puff of smoke had passed by. Mum had no substance at all. Poor Mum. She had been broken in the bud and had never faced her pain. I saw that clearly now. Mum was numb, like my feet and hands. Mum had stopped crying but had not addressed her pain. She did not want to accompany me to a consultation with Vossberg, nor did she want to go with me to Tomato-chan.

Tomato-chan and I were now meditating side by side, Zen-style.
In the second hour, we practised fully formed *kanji* characters.
During the first two years, we practised *kaisho*, the formal square form which 'did not face you but stood with its shoulder turned to you'.
In the third year, we began practising *gyosho* running script.
We embarked on *sosho*, the nearly abstract free form, in the fourth year.
The rituals never changed: the setting up of the the tatami mat with the *zabuton*, the sagging cheeks, the breathing.
An egg timer had replaced the bamboo clapper. We both let out a sharp scream when it rang.
Putting away of the tatami and the zabuton.
Moving to the calligraphy table on our knees over the tatami.
Filling of the ink stone, the grinding of the ink, the strokes...black to grey...sharp as knives...
Put, pull, stop, lift...
Move on to the next stroke...
Stealing of the rejects (I had hundreds of them).

Green tea...
Conversations about swimming.

When it became apparent that there was progress in my condition after reading John Sarno's book, I began to do further research. This was not easy in a country where I could barely read, but there was an English language floor in Kinokuniya, the giant bookstore in Shinjuku.

I read everything on psychology I could get my hands on. *The Drama of the Gifted Child* by Alice Miller; *If You Meet the Buddha on the Road, Kill Him*; *Zen and the Art of Motorcycle Maintenance*; *On Grief and Grieving* by Elisabeth Kübler-Rosss....

Crowds and Power by Elias Canetti had a profound effect on me. In it, Canetti describes how people become parents while they have spears stuck in their bodies. These spears are put there by *their* parents. When the new parents succeed in pulling out the spears, they don't know what to do with them and therefore plant them in the bodies of *their* children, ad infinitum...

Vossberg made me aware of Help!, an off-shoot of *Inochi no Denwa*, a lifeline where I engaged in a six-week training for telephone counsellors.

A world unknown unlocked itself—a world with its jargon. My numb hands, I learned, were called "hysteric gloves" by Freud. I read everything by Freud then. It took me quite a while to understand what a woman-hating wanker Freud really was, but one must start somewhere.

At Help! I met a Japanese-American family therapist and did several courses exploring genograms. It gave me a first glimpse into what they call in Buddhism: "the Wheel of Samsara"; the endless chain of entropy. Tomato-chan had spoken at length about it. It seemed a concept that was deeply ingrained in Japanese culture. The Japanese *expect* to suffer.

Family therapy tells a story of how external forces define a family's dynamics: earthquakes, wars, floods and other natural disasters. During the sessions, I tried to understand Dad as a child of World War II. I tried to understand Mum as a child of the War too.

I tried to understand Agata, papa Daan, mama Sonja, Flaxen...all within their unique genograms. Catholicism had formed them. Catholicism was their natural disaster.

Agata was my natural disaster.

I did not understand yet that I had to understand myself before I could understand anybody else.

I tried to forgive but had not yet forgiven myself.

Vossberg did not let go of me easily. I went to therapy once a week for years after the Spirit of the Fox had left me. My story needed to be told and retold. Slowly we circled the present and the separation from my children. We agreed that I had to get to know better the woman Flaxen was now married to. Thus, when I was well enough, two and a half years after going to the cinema to see *The Taste of Water*, I booked a trip to Europe. I had not seen my children for all that time. We were estranged by time and by our grief.

In Europe, I discovered that Mum and Said were regularly involved in the lives of the new family that my children were now part of. Mum had never said a word about that while she was in Japan.

Mum called Flaxen's wife "a brave little woman". Mum always called other women *vrouwtje* (little women), and so did Agata, when I come to think of it.

I was so nervous to meet the "brave little woman" again that my hands were shaking and numb.

Kunikaze and I were staying in a hotel in Ghent.

Flaxen and his "little woman" lived in the studio that Papa Daan had never occupied. The little woman's name was Brigitte. She was pregnant with her second child. I had brought pairs of baby socks from Japan as presents.

When she opened the door, I immediately understood that Flaxen had married his mother. Brigitte was as petit and flat-chested as Mama Sonja, concave and undercooled. She was not unfriendly and even made us a cup of coffee. She was still wearing her pyjamas. A small child was sitting in a highchair. It resembled my children strongly.

It was clear that Brigitte had Flaxen under control because he was "at work". I could not remember a time when Flaxen was "at work". When he came "home for lunch from work", I could not believe how he had changed. He was a gentleman now, slightly overweight, the kind of man who wears a shawl and uses his overcoat as a cape, arms dangling free. His hair had gone white and was short and combed backward. He wore shoes that he would never have worn before. He was still handsome but in a Richard Gere kind of way. Actually, he resembled Richard Gere quite a lot. This thought caused me a nervous giggling attack, and I told him, who was so familiar to me but whom I could not touch anymore:

"You look like Richard Gere."

"Yeah, er, listen, Shan, enough of your tricks already," he said.

Enough of your tricks. What was that supposed to mean?

I looked around and saw all my old things. They were using all the stuff that once had been mine. I even saw a skirt of mine on a hanger near the ironing board in a corner. Brigitte was wearing my clothes. The cup I drank from had been mine. The kitchen was full of stuff that had been mine. How had they not replaced them? How did they live in the remnants of my former life?

The children came home from school. They had grown so much. They were awkward around Kunikaze and me and did not want my embrace. The presents we had brought were too childish. I felt awful.

Kunikaze had no clue what was going on and sat in the tension with an interested smile as if observing baboons.

I gave Brigitte the socks from Japan. She lay them on the table without a glance.

"Flaxen has an exhibition opening tomorrow night," she said. "You should come."

"An exhibition of what?" I asked.

"Of his furniture," she said.

Flaxen did not say much at all. He sat and ate and drank wine.

Brigitte gave me a flyer. Lo and behold. He had finally done it. He had produced proper furniture.

"You've done it," I said.

"Are you surprised?" Flaxen asked, his eyebrows raised.

The children returned to school, and Flaxen returned to "work" wherever that was.

I did not want to stay alone with Brigitte and Kunikaze.

"We'll be there," I said, waving the brochure.

Once outside in the streets, Kunikaze said the children were *kawaii*.

"If there is one thing my children are not, Kunikaze, it is goddamned *cute*," I said while we walked through the city to our hotel.

Kunikaze blinked, confused. He walked around like a tourist, face turned upwards, admiring the ancient facades. This, unreasonably, irritated the hell out of me.

We passed the house that Flaxen, Sebastiaan and I had once renovated. "The children's birth house," I explained.

The front door was still the same. It had never been painted then and had never been painted since. I looked up at the chimney I had built and thought of long ago when I had stood on the roof, pregnant, and how a cranky old man had called out to me from the street....

How could I even begin to explain these things to Kunikaze?

Kunikaze looked at the house in confusion. Old things were bad in his view. "How can one want to live in such an old house?" he wondered.

I did not explain. A large gap was forming between Kunikaze and me. His Japaneseness irritated me.

At Flaxen's exhibition opening, Brigitte was wearing a leather pair of pants, a pair of staggeringly high heels and much lipstick. She stood by

Flaxen's side as if he were her possession, just like Mama Sonja used to do with Papa Daan. Brigitte behaved like Flaxen's manager and talked about the pieces they were showing with arty-looking businessmen.

I nearly had a giggle attack as I seemed caught in a picture that both Flaxen and I had once despised. Flaxen was walking around awkwardly, drinking one glass of champagne after another, resembling a fat rabbit.

The furniture that was on display was... What did I think of it?

An aluminium cupboard with sliding doors, a wooden coffee table on wheels...

I did not recognise Flaxen in it all. It was ostentatious minimalism. The brochure said it was not minimalist but 'essential'. Whatever that meant. Sure, there were Japanese influences, but the stuff lacked... what? I sat down in some chairs he had designed. They were cold to the touch and uncomfortable. Form over function. He had not worked them through. They were born too early... We used to talk about such things...

I suddenly noticed how little interested I was. Why sit in a house with this stuff around you when you could be in a city like Tokyo? Why try to impress your friends with these pieces? Who the fuck wanted a designer's coffee table in the first place? It seemed all so stupid to me. The only thing I liked was one chair. It was not clear how it held itself up. It had to be X-rayed to understand the concept. The chair had a skeleton, like a human or an animal. It was held upright and strong by its bones and bent under the weight of the sitter. With its construction parts out of the way, it was extremely thin and light. This was unique and new.

I looked around for Flaxen to tell him my thoughts, but he was standing with Mama Sonja, Papa Daan, and Brigitte. They ignored me, although I thought I saw a glimmer of acknowledgement on Papa Daan's face. He sort of took his hat off to me. It could have been an illusion. He was drunk, as usual, which I could tell from the swaying of his upper body. Flaxen was drunk too. It was embarrassing. He was slurring his words. It was clear from their standing together that Brigitte had been firmly accepted into the family. They formed a tasteful lot. That is what it was all about; taste. Brigitte fit in their interiors. How could I have ever expected that it would be different? Papa Daan and Mama Sonja were all about taste: a façade.

I decided not to play the Face Game. I walked straight to Brigitte and said: "Hey, any chance I can have my children back?"

She looked down at me from her platformed heels.

"As I have said before: They are not suitcases that you can just move from one country to another, you know," she said, turning her back on me.

I knew she was right.

I did not try hard to get the children back. I thought that if they were meant to be with me, this would happen in its own way. It had taken too long to recover from the Spirit of the Fox. There were too many good things about their situation, although it was far from ideal. They were raised in a family and went to school in their own language. I could not offer them that. They had already become thoroughly Flemish and had forgotten their Japanese. It would not be easy for them to uproot. I had their well-being in mind and not my own. Although it broke my heart, I decided not to fight for them. I had to let them go. Again.

"Your companion looks nice," Brigitte said when the wine flowed, and the tension subsided somewhat.

"Yes, he's nice," I lied.

Kunikaze was looking lost in the crowd. He had no clue of what was going on.

After Ghent, I took the children and Kunikaze to visit my family. We went by train. David asked why we didn't go by car.

"I can't drive," I said. "We don't need cars in Tokyo. Don't you remember the trains we took? Don't you remember how you jumped in a train and Hannes and I were left on the platform?"

They could only vaguely remember it.

They giggled over the fact that I could not drive a car.

During the train ride, Hannes said: "Brigitte must go."

My heart cracked in two, but I said firmly: "No, Papa is with her now and not with me."

They wanted me to tell stories about the past.

I told them about Hannes's rubber addiction:

"When Hannes was a couple of hours old, he started sucking his thumb. The other fingers were in the air, rubbing each other. When we came home, and I put him in his crib, he scrunched up the sheet with his fingers and took the rubber sheet underneath it in his hand. He seemed to like to softness of the rubber between his fingers and the smell of the rubber.

When he was older, he took the rubber sheet everywhere. It got filthy, and he would not let me wash it. I had several in stock because he would not sleep without one.

When he began to walk, he would lose half of it, then a quarter, until he was three or so, only needed a sliver of the rubber between his fingers. There were slivers of rubber everywhere throughout the house. When he was tired, he would scoop one up with the hand of which his thumb was already in his mouth.

We had to ensure we took enough rubber slivers with us when we went somewhere overnight because he would not sleep without one. We once forgot to take the slivers to a sleepover at Bonma and Bonpa.

We tried all sorts of rubber; we cut up a bathing cap and an inner tube of a bicycle... nothing worked. We had to drive back to Ghent in the dead of night.

It was only in Japan that Hannes decided it had been enough. He gathered all the slivers and put them in the bin.

He took one out of the bin again at night, but the next night he did not. He was five years old then."

The children listened, their eyes wide, and laughed. Although they were constantly fighting, they were close. They had each other. This put my mind at ease somewhat.

First, we visited Dad, who praised me for being brave and being friends with Brigitte, that brave little woman.

"She's not my friend," I said.

Agata also remarked on what a brave little woman Brigitte was.

Fuck off with your little women, I thought. I was not enjoying our stay because I now knew and *felt* how angry I was at them.

Kunikaze had no clue what was happening and said they were "nice."

They ignored Kunikaze once they discovered he did not engage in conversation because his English was not good enough, and he did not understand who was who.

"Are these children your sisters and brothers?"

"No, they are the children of my father's third wife."

Kunikaze scratched his head and disengaged. He patiently waited for me to take him sightseeing.

I felt exhausted.

I told Dad and Agata: "We should seek family therapy."

"You are Americanised. We do not believe in therapy".

I wondered how I would get through the rest of the visit when something surprising happened on the second day. The doorbell rang. Dad went to open the door. He came back with a man in tow. The man said:

"Hello, Shan."

I had no idea who he was and looked at him long and puzzled.

"How are you?"

I knew that voice. Suddenly it clicked. It was Dick, one of my old friends from Amersfoort. He had doubled in size.

"Dick!" I said. "How did you know I was here?"

"I didn't."

He told us how he and his wife had lost a baby and how he was compelled by grief to investigate his parents' past, who were from Harlingen, the harbour town where Dad and Agata now lived.

He had vaguely remembered that Dad had moved here and had asked around: a painter, a musician... Hendrik, father of Shan. It had not taken long to find him; everyone knew Dad; he played in the local cafés, solo, and in Jazz bands.

I introduced Dick to my children and Kunikaze. We walked along the seashore while Dick spoke about the loss of his child. He had not heard that Flaxen and I had split or that I lived in Japan.

"What an extraordinary coincidence that I am here just when you came looking," I said. "How is everyone? Are you still in touch?"

"I am still in touch with Ellie and Wilco", he said. "Shall I put you in touch?"

"Yes, please," I said. "What about Fransje?"

"I am not sure if it is true," Dick said, "but I've heard he is dead."

We walked on in silence while the children were practising jumps and poses from The Karate Kid.

Fransje dead? How could that be?

"Why don't we go out for dinner, the four of us in Amsterdam," said Dick, "for old times sake."

"That sounds awesome!"

The children and Kunikaze stayed home with Mum and Said when I went for dinner in Amsterdam with the old gang. Nobody knew how Hansje was and what became of her, and nobody was sure about Fransje's fate. Could he really be dead? That dynamo of a boy! He did drugs, and he was fearless when he took them. But he preferred mushrooms, and how could one die from that? Had he eaten the wrong one, that poisoned him?

I never found out and do not know to this day.

Ellie and Mother Oak had not changed. They were cheerful and kind. But Wilco, mama mia, just like Dick, had doubled in size. He was tall and already nearly bald. He had been girlish and thin, and his hair had been curly and long the last time I had seen him, years ago. Now he wore a suit and a tie. He was the ugliest bloke one could imagine, he resembled a tarantula with his hairy arms, but he was sharp like before, but boy, did they like their drinks, Wilco and Dick!

But then, we all liked to bend the elbow; the wine flowed, and the conversation was great. Mother Oak still cleaned at *Contact der Continenten* and went to Russia every second year. She still occupied the tiny house.

Ellie had studied city planning and worked at the council of Amersfoort.

Dick and Wilco had dropped out of university and worked in Amsterdam in office jobs they did not want to discuss.

I told them about Tokyo and Kunikaze, and they all promised to come and visit one day. I was in Europe several times a year to see the children so we could meet again. Late that night, I told them about the Spirit of the Fox over a nightcap in a nightclub. They listened. They understood.

When I arrived at Mum's the next day, Said and Kunikaze had gone to the market. The children were seated at the dinner table, a light blue manual typewriter in front of them. Hannes was typing with one finger while David was reading what he typed, shrieking with laughter. A pile of paper was handed to me. They were "threatening letters" addressed to me.

Esteemed Mama

We want skateboards and know the shop where they are for sale here. If you do not go with us and buy us new skateboards, we will shackle you to a bicycle, and you must ride it until you fall. We will then drag you through the gravel and pour vinegar on the wounds.
Sincerely yours, David

Honourable Mama

If we do not get skate shirts too, we will lock you in the garage without light, food, or water for a week. Then, when we open the garage, we will put clamps on your eyelids so that you must keep your eyes open in the blinding light. We hope that this convinces you to buy two sweatshirts of the trademark Vision. Thank you.

Warm regards Hannes

Said and Kunikaze came in, their hands full of shopping bags. They seemed to get along well. I looked at Said with the letters in my hand.

"You are behind this, I gather?"

Said grinned.

It did not stop at that. In their bedroom, they had found my old Barbie dolls. With the help of Said, they had crucified them with tiny nails through their feet and hands against the door of the wardrobe.

"Look at the feet," said David, "they are perfect for crucifixion."

The Barbie dolls hung there for a few days with their messed-up hair and ripped clothes. The children were lame with laughter every time they saw them, and so was Said.

Kunikaze had no clue of what was going on.

"What the hell?" I said to Mum.

Mum shrugged. "Men!" she said.

Three weeks of Flaxen and Brigitte, Dad and Agata, Dad's third wife, the chemist and her offspring as the newest addition to the family, and Mum and Said was enough to strongly long for my newly won sanity in Tokyo.

How I wanted to take the children with me! I fantasised about kidnapping them. Strangely, saying goodbye seemed not to bother them much.

Kunikaze and I walked them to school, where they dissolved into a sea of friends, romping, laughing, and frolicking.

I waved.

They did not look back.

I welcomed the descent of the plane over Tokyo and the now familiar blue roof tiles of the houses. I imagined how I showed the children: *Look! The roofs are blue here.*

I imagined the children in the Japanese educational system. I thought about Japanese babies who spent all their time in a sling on their mother's backs and slept in bed with their mothers. I wished I had done that. Why waste time with a frisky husband when you can sleep with your gorgeous children? I reckoned it was good for them. Japanese children seemed content, at least when they were small.

They were seen as little gods in the same realm as old people. This lovely life ended abruptly when school began, where they were groomed for a future of work. Uniformity was given. They were released from the iron grip of school and career only when they were old and became gods again.

Could I do that to my children?

No.

Could I afford to send them to an international school?

No.

Was Kunikaze capable of raising children?

No.

The answer was clear; I had made the right decision by leaving them behind. I closed my eyes before the tears could escape. I had to carve my new way into the world.

Before I went back to Help!, I had booked a retreat in a Zen monastery for a couple of weeks. My love affair with Zen began when I studied with Tomato-chan and deepened on Mount Takao West of Tokyo, where I encountered a group of monks sitting under a waterfall. The water rammed their bald heads. When their meditation was over, they walked to their monastery using the same path I was on, chatting and laughing softly. They were old men. Their faces were made of light.

Their wrinkles pointed upwards like the sun's rays in a child's drawing. They seemed kind and unhurried. This short moment had a profound effect. I wanted to become like them. I also felt a similarity: they were lovers that are alone. They remained apart, like water and oil, even when surrounded by people. Yet, they spoke the language of love. But I did not want to be part of their institution. I wanted to be like Tomato-chan—a nun in the wild.

I arrived at four in the morning at the gate of the Rinzai monastery and was welcomed by a guide who led me over the polished floor of an outdoor dojo to a second gate. A large field of mountain river gravel stretched in front of us. On the gravel, near the door of the next building, sat a man on his knees, his forehead against the gravel.

"What is he doing there?" I asked.

"He is waiting to be admitted as a monk," said the guide.

The door in the building slid open, and a monk in a grey kimono stepped out with a long wooden stick in his hand. He struck the prostrating man on the shoulder. The victim stretched his back and rubbed his shoulders. The man with the stick hit again. Bang, on the other shoulder of the man. This time the man got up and rubbed both shoulders while the monk went back inside.

"What did he do that for?" I asked, shocked.

"It is part of the admission process," said the guide. "It doesn't hurt much; besides, it gives the kneeler an excuse to get up and stretch."

"Will I have to go through this "ceremony" too?" I asked.

The guide laughed: "No, only novices do."

I wondered what else was watered down for external students.

We bypassed the building where the man was prostrating and went to a small wooden building behind it.

This is where the women lived. They, too, had those faces. Faces of lovers without a subject. I knew what I was or wanted to be: a nun in the wild. These calm women were entirely asexual.

I realised that all the sex I had encountered till then, when I was thirty-three years old, I had not liked it. I did not like sex at all, but, contrary to other non-conventional sexual orientation groups like gays and transvestites, there was no social group for asexuals, except in monasteries.

Perhaps Dad had taken my ability to like sex that evening long ago; perhaps it had happened earlier; perhaps it had been like this for me all along, since the incubator... it did not matter. A lover without a subject, I would be.

I spent four weeks with the nuns. It reminded me of the Maijuku course.

We rose early at the sharp sound of a bell and ran barefoot over the ice-cold wooden floors with a rag to clean the shiny planks. We washed our faces slowly with ice-cold water. Mindfulness was required to slowly cover the whole skull: ears, eyes, nose, cheeks, head, and neck.

It was followed by twenty minutes of zazen.

Another bell invited us to breakfast, a meal of miso soup, vegetables, tofu, and green tea, that was eaten in silence.

After a second zazen, we split up into groups to do chores. I liked helping in the kitchen, especially with rice washing. There was something satisfying about rinsing the clouds of starch away with the water from a creek nearby and not letting one grain of rice escape.

I observed my monkey mind, how it jumped from branch to branch, never stopping, never resting, on and on. My stampeding elephant...

Had the nuns and monks with the light faces stopped thinking altogether, I wondered? This seemed incredible and not quite right. Listening to the teachings, I understood they were after living in the here and now. When one reached that goal, one was enlightened.

I wondered whether the spells I had experienced since childhood were spells of enlightenment or, instead, the opposite, spells of escape from the here and now. It was difficult to say. One day I saw it this way; the other day, that way. I tried to talk about it with the nun who oversaw us. She said I was to observe myself and the others.

"Just sit," she said.

I made a mental note to discuss the spells with Vossberg.

At lunch, one of the nuns hit a large wooden fish, which hung from the ceiling, with a wooden bat.

Bang!

It was the sign that we could begin eating.

In the afternoons, we observed the men asking questions to an Elder in a yellow robe seated on a wooden highchair. He gave crazy answers to questions or told crazy little stories, *koan*, that would 'break the mind'.

"Does a dog have Buddha nature?"

"*Mu*. (Empty)"

"What is enlightenment?"

"The Oaktree in the garden."

"What is the nature of reality?"

He put his finger to his lips and said: "sssssh".

"Kensha lost his faith and left the monastery. He walked away, and on the path from the monastery, he hit his toe against a rock and had a profound awakening.

He limped back to the monastery, and a monk asked:

'Why did you come back?'

Kensha answered: "Not a single step was taken. The whole universe is one bright pearl.'"

We practised "beginner's mind" when at koan practice. The simple practice is that we are part of constant newness. We were invited to ask ourselves the following questions:

"Who am I"

"What is this?"

"Who is it, dragging around this corpse?"

"What is my original face from before my parents were born?"

"Joshu asked: 'What is the way?'

Nanzen answered: 'Ordinary mind is the way.'

'Should I turn towards it?'

'If you turn towards it, you turn against it.'

'If I can't look for it, how do I find it?'

Nanzen answers: 'The way is not about knowing or not knowing. It is as vast and empty as the wide-open sky when you find it. It is all-pervasive. It is already here. It is not on the level of the questions being asked. It is not an answer. We are not apart from it.'"

As the weeks progressed, we were to imagine our death and how our body fell apart until nothing was left of it. This was called the Meditation of the Charnel Grounds. First, we imagined our bodies still, pale, and without a life force. Then, a day or two into the process, the body becomes spotty and reeks. A couple of days later, holes are formed and black patches. Gasses escape. Days later, maggots are crawling everywhere, eating the rotting flesh. Flies cover the corps and produce a regular noise as if a small motor is running. The muscles become visible, and the yellow bones. One cannot approach without gagging and vomiting. The muscles are eaten off the bone by animals, and the bones dry up and turn white and brittle and are scattered by animals and the wind.

I asked how this mediation was as it was, as the Japanese have no burials, only cremation.

"Buddhism originated in India. But it does not matter," said the teacher. Smart-ass questions were not appreciated and ignored or sidestepped like this.

After my stay at the monastery, Help! played an increasingly significant role in my life.

I became a telephone counsellor. The course, given by American mental health professionals, had been a first glance into my dysfunctions. Manning the telephones, I learned what private hells other people live in and that what I had experienced was not that special. The nuclear family seemed the source of a particular hell, with subtle tortures often encouraged by society.

I continued going to Vossberg for mental hygiene. After the Spirit of the Fox had retreated into its nest or burrow, I presented him with a stack of Chinese 'money', gold blade on washi, to symbolise that no money could ever repay him for what he had done for me.

"Without you, I would have died."

He received the gift humbly and was somewhat confused by its meaning. Later I learned that, in Japan, this 'money' was used to burn with the dead to provide them with money to travel to wherever the dead travel. Whether Vossberg knew this or not, I never found out. As time passed, I learned to look lightly at the Spirit of the Fox, as an extreme form of TMS.

I told Vossberg about the spells I experienced in childhood. He said:

"If there are no physical reasons for a child experiencing spells and leaving their body, such as seizures, it is likely to be a symptom of a psychological or psychiatric condition. Here are a few possibilities: Dissociative disorders: which involves a disconnection or detachment from one's thoughts, feelings, memories, or identity. Children with dissociative disorders may experience leaving their bodies or feeling like they are observing themselves from a distance. Panic attacks: these are sudden and intense episodes of fear or discomfort that can cause physical symptoms such as chest pain, rapid heartbeat, sweating, and shaking. Children with panic disorder may experience spells where they feel like they are losing control or are detached from reality. Anxiety disorders: Children with anxiety disorders may experience physical symptoms such as rapid heartbeat, sweating, and trembling in response to a perceived threat. These symptoms can sometimes be severe and feel like a spell. Trauma and stress-related disorders such as post-traumatic stress disorder can cause flashbacks, nightmares, and dissociation in children who have experienced or witnessed a traumatic event. Psychotic disorders: Psychotic disorders such as schizophrenia can cause hallucinations and delusions that may make a child feel like they are leaving their body or experiencing things that are not real."

"It is too late for that now," I said. Agata used to give me sugared water.

Vossberg made a noise with his throat that indicated disdain and disbelief.

"I am all for not medicalising a child's condition, but to never consult a professional when a child experiences these symptoms and is capable of expressing them, is neglect in my world," he said.

I learned how much death is seen as 'travel' in Japan when Kunikaze's mother died. I had seen the movie *O Soshiki* (The Funeral) by Juso Itami and was now treated to a similar real-life scene. The corpse of the woman I had never known was transported to Kunikaze's brother's home, where Yukie and other women had to wash it and dress it in a white kimono for the travel ahead. The dead feet were dressed in white *tabi* and rope sandals for the road ahead. The corpse was displayed, covered in flowers, in a hall in Kunitachi. A table and black and white banners and flags were placed at the front entrance, where money was given in envelopes with golden decorations.

The wake went on for three days in the heat of summer, and the face of the corpse, which was the only part visible, caved in further every day. The body was transported to a black marble cremation hall, where the flames consumed it.

After the burning, we walked around a stainless-steel table to pick up the hot bones with long chopsticks and place them in an urn. The skull cap went on top, then the throat bone, which is supposed to look like a Buddha. The ashes were brushed away with a brush and dustpan and poured between the bones.

We then piled in cars and had dinner at a local restaurant where one chair was reserved for the deceased and where she was served the same food as we were, 'for the journey'.

I yearned to learn, not only from experience but formally too. It had just become possible to attend university by correspondence course. I enrolled in the bachelor's course of Social Sciences at the Open University in the Netherlands.

At the same time, I was offered a full-time job at Help! to help to coordinate the training and the telephone counsellors' shifts. My managers were American ministers and pastoral counsellors who worked for the American churches around Tokyo. They organised food vans for the poor, managed shelters, and counselled the bereaved… They were fantastic people from whom I learned what compassion was.

My direct boss was Bob Eades, who taught Bible classes. I loved Bob and his wife, Dee. They were humble people. I enrolled in Bob's classes to be near him and was grateful that Dad had taught us the Bible when we were small. I knew quite a lot. Learning more about the foundations of my own culture while living in one so foreign was soothing.

Through all these experiences, I grew into the person I was supposed to be, a citizen of the world who spoke the language of love. I did not subscribe to any religion but studied religions seriously, Zen and Christianity and the great mystics, and I did not feel conflicted about it.

I discussed with Bob Eades how I thought God had moved further away from people. First, she was in trees, in the toilet, and in the kitchen, like Japanese Shinto gods, later she could be found in the sky, and now she was somewhere at the verges of the universe, where we had not had the opportunity to explore yet. We discussed these things while folding flyers for the ever-expanding organisation or setting up the training room.

I felt at home at work and happy. I met people I am in touch with until this day, for example, the woman with the flaming red hair, Belinda, coordinator of training, who gave me the idea for my first book, *The Japanese Riddle*, and Carrie, coordinator of volunteers, with whom I went dancing in tiny salsa bars all night to go to work the next day without having slept, our clothes smelling of smoke and booze.

For the first time, I experienced that life can be good and can be celebrated. I understood that my existence was separate from my unasked-for bonus families, that I was free.

WOMEN!

While I was flourishing, Flaxen was going downhill quickly. Every time I visited the children, he became more of an asshole. He looked like a giant baby. He was drinking like a fish. His furniture was being shown and sold everywhere in Europe, but this was due to Brigitte, who managed him and his work.

I looked at Brigitte, who had two small children and felt sorry for her. She was the ultimate example of a Willing Slave of the West. She held two jobs, looked after four children, and managed a baby-man. She lived in the pockets of a mother-in-law who could not stay out of her son's life. Flaxen had bought the building next to Mama Sonja, an old school. In the same whining voice as Mama Sonja, Brigitte nagged Flaxen to finish the renovations, which, unsurprisingly, he never did.

I began to make plans again in case I had to take the children out of his vicinity.

There would come a time when he would become as useless as Papa Daan.

Flaxen came home drunk occasionally to shout at his wife that she had become his second mama Sonja. I was glad I had spent the best years of his life with him when he was still lovely and sane, like any young person. I felt that he would die soon. Drive himself to a pulp, overdose...

Visiting Mum and Said was becoming a chore too. Said was unhappy in his job, and Mum was spending his salary as if she was married to a medical specialist instead of a scholar. They lived far beyond their means. Said double-mortgaged the house because of it. Ultimately, they had to give up the canal house and move into a one-bedroom apartment. Said had to become strict with Mum were they to fund his retirement. Mum went to a course, I think, where she learned to manage money. She even got a part-time job in a French fabric store.

Said resented her for spending all he had worked for. But he had let it happen. He was bitter and sarcastic and talked about Mum behind her back. Mum, quasi-oblivious as always, sat in the kitchen or the living room with a book, feet on the radiator. Their tiny apartment was always organised and clean, and the food was good but not enough consistently. They slept in separate beds with French fabric bedspreads in a small bedroom. There was no room for me and the children, so we paid day visits.

Visiting Dad and the bonus family was increasingly painful too. Dad suffered a second stroke. Agata talked to him as if he was a child. The chemist and her children were weird. I did not want to get to know them better. Dad did recover his ability to play his instruments. We sang to escape the now constant awkwardness between us. I was becoming someone separate from him, and he didn't like it. And I did not know how to express my mounting anger toward him.

18

Rik Schipper, at last

Flo wrote to me in 2021, after I'd sent her this memoir while I was writing it:

Hi Shan

That was a tough piece to read. It gives insight into the events of the time, your choice. And what a horror the way you fell to pieces. What a lonely journey. You were still so young. It occurred to me that all the women I know who have lost a child or their children in one way or another went to pieces.

In the homes of Dad and Mum, there was only talk of 'crazy, she's crazy, she's getting crazier'. And, of course, there was the struggle for Dad's favour. Were you good, or were you bad? You had better be in the good camp.

I once wrote a letter to Dad expressing my concerns about nuclear missiles. In 1983 there was a vast mass demonstration nationwide, the biggest there ever. I was there, I got injured, and I made my first photo series. In the letter, I reproached Dad for not being involved and asked if he was not worried and that I did not understand.

He answered my letter: 'If you attack me with conventional weapons, I will drop a nuclear bomb on you immediately.' Hendrik.

I think I experienced a frozen moment when I read his witty and ice-cold reply.
Flo
December 2021

Whenever I tried to talk with Dad about the past, he said, "If you attack me with conventional weapons, I will drop a nuclear bomb on you immediately."

In that one sentence, he summed up exactly what he had always done: If we disagreed with him, he nuked us.

When Kunikaze and I were staying with Dad with the children that year, Dad was sitting in the living room, reading the weekly magazine *Vrij Nederland* (Free Holland), when he jumped up and began pacing while reading. He seemed to be crying. I asked what the matter was.

"I have just found a long-lost brother," he said and showed me the article he was reading.

The article was about Rik Schipper.

When reading that name, old memories came flooding back. Rik Schipper. When I was small, this name had been on everyone's lips. Rik Schipper had been raised by Oma V after the war. He had suddenly disappeared. Postcards from all over the world had arrived.

I had not heard the name for a long time, but it all came back to me now. I could again smell the parsonage where Oma V had lived. I thought about how Oma V and Uncle Arne had moved away from that magnificent place next to the church into a newly built neighbourhood where all the houses were the same. They had not lasted long. First, Oma V had died, and a month or so later, Uncle Arne.

Dad had an icy attitude to his mother and Uncle Arne's deaths:

"They are at the Eternal Hunting Grounds now, and I never think about them," he said.

Both Oma V and Uncle Arne are buried in the tiny graveyard next to the parsonage, and their graves are seldom visited.

It was strange that this article about Rik Schipper moved Dad so. But that was Dad. Either black or white.

After he was done with the article, his pacing and his crying, he handed the magazine to me.

It described Rik Schipper by his Chinese name Shi Zhouren, a Dutch sinologist who had studied the ceremonies and rituals of Taoism in Taiwan. A family adopted him so that he could be trained in Taoism. In 1968 he was initiated as a priest in the Zhengyi School. He had worked on the first complete scientific study of the fifteen hundred works in the Ming Dynasty's Taoist Canon. He had made Taoism his life's work, helping to uplift it from folklore to a religious tradition. He described how Chinese society has been organised, throughout its history, by local groups centred around temples rather than the emperor and his bureaucracy.

As an ordained Taoist priest, he combined practical knowledge of rural religious life with studying classical Chinese. He showed that there was a religion of the people of China that was deeply connected to local forms of self-organisation and self-government.

Dad and Rik had lived together when Dad was a teenager. Rik, who was older than Dad, had been instrumental in discovering that Dad was good at drawing. He had also introduced Dad to Jazz music.

Dad was on the phone with *Vrij Nederland* to see if he could meet with Rik. He succeeded in getting an appointment while Rik was still in the Netherlands. I was returning to Tokyo while Dad was in the midst of it. The meeting had been a success, wrote Dad. Rik was about to go to Tokyo, where he wanted to meet me. Dad had ripped a picture of himself in half and sent one part to me and one to Rik, so we could match them when we met.

I met Rik in a coffee house in Shimokitazawa. He was already seated. I recognised him from the photos in *Vrij Nederland*. It was a giant coffee house. I had to slalom between tables to reach him. I pulled half of the photo of Dad from my handbag. Rik's half lay in front of him on the table.

"You must be Rik Schipper," I said while fitting my half of the photo to his. "I have been wanting to meet you since I was three."

He looked at me while he was holding my two hands in his.

"You look exactly like your grandmother," he said.

"Really?"

"A spitting image."

I sat down opposite him, and we ordered coffee. This man had known my family before it fell apart.

"You must tell me all about Oma V," I said. "And about you. I have been your distant admirer for so long."

He laughed. "And why is that?"

"Because you went away and did something amazing."

Rik agreed to come to the apartment where I lived with Kunikaze. He was entirely at ease with Japanese customs. He was a large red-headed man but moved like an Asian person. He could read Japanese, and we looked at the beautiful kanji dictionaries I had collected.

He told us about China and Taiwan and how Taoism was a living religion. He was pleasantly soft-spoken. He invited Kunikaze and me to a ceremony at the famous Asakusa shrine the next day. Kunikaze declined the invitation because he had to work. I cancelled all my obligations to witness Rik in full ceremonial dress calmy perform a ceremony in the inner part of the shrine.

We went there by train. We spoke about so many things; the conversation was lively and kaleidoscopic. I loved this man. He was focused on just one thing: the Tao temples of China and their stories, the people that gathered and organised themselves around them.

I told him I had been trying to write a book since I was ten. I always embarked on one and then lost my way in its complexity.

"It's because you don't focus on a steady subject. Just write about your life as a Japanese housewife," he said.

WOMEN!

I was stunned. Was that how he saw me? A housewife? I had done so many things and survived so many wars. A housewife? Really? Maybe he was right. I had no titles. I was nothing in particular. And when one is nothing in particular and a woman, one is a housewife, a Willing Slave of the West. How bloody awful!

We talked about the Netherlands. Rik, like I, did not like the Netherlands. The Netherlands is called *Nederland* in Dutch. He called it *vernederland*, which can mean *far Nederland* or *humiliation land*.

I agreed with him. I, too, felt humiliated in and by that little arrogant country that lies between England, France, and Germany like a little screaming brat, a tiny braggart, a minuscule flat accident.

Like me, Rik had sought his fortune in a faraway place and had succeeded.

I wanted to talk with Rik about Dad, but when I tried, I found that Rik admired Dad's ventures into polygamy. He was a fan of Dad and his social experiments and had even gone so far as to buy a boat, as Dad had after our unfortunate trip across the North Sea in a Cornish Crabber.

I had hoped that Rik could be instrumental in getting my family together for some therapy, but I had to abandon this idea.

Instead, I told him how fragmented we had become. I had not seen Lilibeth or Flo in ages. They were not interested in what I was doing. Flo was a mother obsessed with her children and smothered them. Lilibeth was a contact lens maker and lived with a pianist. I only saw Dad and Mum because of the children, and although Dad showed little interest in them, Mum had grown slightly warmer and tried to be a good Oma. She even used words like "darling" and "dear child". Said played wicked games with them, like writing me threatening letters and crucifying Barbie dolls.

Exhausted from these visits, I gladly retreated to Japan, the home to the largest economic bubble in the world's history, to that fabulous, almost unbelievable amount of energy, wealth, technology, and a feeling it was about to take over the world. Japanese cars went from cheap little imports to a threat to the American automobile industry, electronics pushed all competitors out of business, and the Japanese seemed relentlessly focused on going up and up. By 1985 there was a real hope that Japan would own the next generation of computing, chip manufacturing, and robotics.

Everyone worked hard, much harder than Westerners could even imagine.

Interest rates were cut drastically and kept recreating the boom, now fuelled by cheap money. First came the property boom, and then came the stock market boom. The market more than tripled.

Instead of buckling under the high yen, Japan went up and up the technology ladder, dominating one industry after another with rational long-term planning. At the same time, Western countries were obsessed only with the short term.

The strong yen, instead of an impediment, only further strengthened Japan's position. Everyone thought this scenario was entirely plausible. Companies went from strength to strength. Nine out of the world's ten largest banks were Japanese.

By 1989, Japanese banks supplied twenty per cent of all credit in California; Nomura Securities was said to have enough capital to purchase all Wall Street investment banks; Japanese households saved an average of seventeen per cent of their income; the Japanese Postal Service had assets greater than the twelve largest American banks combined; the Greater Tokyo area had a GDP larger than that of the entire UK; the Tokyo Imperial Palace alone, sitting on one square kilometre of land was estimated to have a value greater than all the land in California. Despite Japan occupying the equivalent of only four per cent of America's land area, the Japanese property market was worth four times more than the American property market.

Golf club memberships became a tradable commodity. Japanese executives had long been famous for their love of golf, and membership in Japan's most expensive golf courses could cost more than three million US dollars.

Pachinko parlours with pinball machines were so popular that they had an annual revenue larger than the entire South Korean GDP.

Investors owned forty-five per cent of prime real estate in downtown Los Angeles; Japan was the largest foreign investor in the USA and the largest creditor nation on earth; it bought Columbia Pictures (which became Sony Pictures), Pebble Beach Golf Course, and Rockefeller Centre in NYC; and replaced the USA as the world's largest creditor.

I observed and absorbed it all, not yet knowing I was witnessing a unique historical time and place. The strong yen made for a great time shopping and vacationing abroad. We were wealthy and happy, and you would never hear me say that money doesn't make one happy, but there was so much more to it all. The movies from that era, the art galleries, the literature... it all had a vibrancy that was never reached again anywhere afterwards. It was the first time foreigners could stay in Japan for long periods. A mixing of cultures, old and new, was happening.

Rik Schipper had recommended that I write a book about my life 'as a Japanese housewife'. I'd rather cut my wrists! Instead, I began writing short observations about daily life in Tokyo in Dutch and sent them to *Vrij Nederland*. They were accepted immediately and *Vrij Nederland* paid handsomely for them. Initially, three stories with black and white photos by Magnum were published: one about the *yakuza*, one about the *sento* and one about the *mizu shobai*.

I interviewed the filmmaker Juso Itami in the hospital for another article. Members of the yakuza had just attacked him after releasing his anti-yakuza satire *Minbō no Onna*. This attack on the filmmaker's life led to a government crackdown on the yakuza.

His stay in the hospital inspired his next film *Daibyonin* (Big Hospitals), a grim satire on the Japanese health system that I, too, had had a brush with when I began suffering from the Spirit of the Fox. During a movie showing in Tokyo, a right-wing activist slashed a cinema screen.

My articles in *Vrij Nederland* led a respectable publishing house to ask for more stories, and in 1991, I published my first book: *Ichi Go, ichi En*.

Mum was highly interested in the short flash of 'fame' I received in the Netherlands because of the book's release. I was invited to several TV programs, and Mum accompanied me. Sometimes Said came too. Mum would whisper loudly when she encountered famous people while we walked through the corridors in television station buildings. I begged her to stop that embarrassing behaviour. This did not help a bit. Most programs had an audience in the background, seated around tables with glasses of wine and sometimes, the cameras zoomed in on their faces. This is what Mum was hoping for. She loved being in the make-up rooms where a crew powdered her face. Mum had never been so interested in me and has never been since.

I wrote again about Itami when he died in 1997 after falling from the roof of the building where his office was located. On his desk was a suicide note stating that he had been falsely accused of an affair and was taking his life to clear his name. Two days later, a tabloid magazine published a report of the affair. No one, including Itami's family, believed that he had taken his life or would be mortally embarrassed by an affair.

In 2008, a former member of the Goto-gumi yakuza group told a reporter:

"We set it up to stage his murder as a suicide. We dragged him to the rooftop and put a gun in his face. We gave him a choice: jump and you might live, or stay and we'll blow your face off. He jumped. He didn't live."

I now was something other than a housewife and a Willing Slave of the West. I was a writer. A writer!

19

Huis ten Bosch, Nagasaki

The Economic Bubble burst in 1990. First, the stock market blew up, and then real estate prices collapsed. It was a rapid demise.

By 2004, commercial real estate prices in Tokyo had declined to less than one per cent of their peak value in the eighties, and Tokyo residential real estate prices declined to less than ten per cent of their peak in the eighties.

This was the beginning of Japan's Lost Decade.

It is worth pausing here and remembering when Japan was number one and the future had no bounds. This optimism rubbed off on everybody. Encouraged by this extraordinary era and the publication of my first book, I decided to write a novel.

In Belgium, Flaxen's decline happened simultaneously with the decline of Japan and was as tragic.

Flaxen entered his 'lost decade' at the same time as Japan did and before he died in 2005 at forty-five.

The press and the design world had propped him and his work up like they once did with his father's contribution to the history of painting. A few pieces of furniture, the chair the only good, were rehashed, remade, and repraised. A cult following was the result.

While Sebastiaan was designing and producing one solid piece of furniture after another and selling them locally in his store, Flaxen's work was surrounded by the jargon of art critics.

Flaxen was seen with various women in the nightclubs in Ghent that were now also frequented by our teenage children. afraid to go out for fear that they might see their father, loosened by cocaine and alcohol, dancing on tables with women who were neither their mother nor their stepmother but were often of an
age similar to their own.

Once again, it was hammered home to me how serious the situation was when Brigitte, the four children, Kunikaze, and I had dinner one evening at their unfinished house. Flaxen came in, high as a kite, and shouted at Brigitte. The children fled from their chairs and flocked to a corner. They huddled there, crouching, like once, a long time ago, Flo and I had in the hallway when Mum cried in the kitchen, and Dad raised his voice.

I had to do something. I had saved up money for the children for years. I was getting more and more writing gigs. I am the only person on earth who decided to write a novel and get rich enough to buy apartments for the children, but that is precisely what happened.

At Help!, my colleague, the flaming redhead Belinda, had said, while we were setting up the training room:

"This place," (Help!) "is perfect for a novel about a serial killer".

I knew immediately what she meant, and an elaborate scenario rolled through my head from beginning to end. All I had to do was write it down. All my friends would play a role in it, and it would be a kaleidoscope of throbbing decadence, sex and luxury, like the broken Dame that Tokyo now was.

I still travelled back and forth between Tokyo and Europe several times a year. Only an economic bubble could cause me to afford such luxury at a time when flying was still a rare and expensive endeavour. We could still smoke cigarettes on aeroplanes and were served incredible meals by Japan Airlines accompanied by silver cutlery and white linen napkins. The air hostesses would come around with excellent wines. We received care packages with bottled water, a blanket, toothpaste and a toothbrush, a box of toothpicks, soap, a towel, and a pair of socks and slippers. It was like being in a hotel. Passengers had a row of chairs each and could sleep. A movie projected onto the wall elevated the boredom.

At Schiphol airport, I was often met by Wilco or Dick to meet up with Elly and Mother Oak in a trendy restaurant in Amsterdam; amongst them, I was well-travelled. Mother Oak still travelled to Russia every two years by Trans Siberia Express.

Dick and Wilco travelled to France or Portugal or Spain, as Northern Europeans do, but not for elaborate holidays like we did with Mum and Dad when I was a child, but rather for a week at the poolside of a hotel, away from their office jobs.

My children were now of an age that they could join us. They liked fine dining.

After a few weeks in the Netherlands, we went to Belgium, where Flaxen's decline was so alarming that his producer regularly put him through expensive rehabs in Switzerland. It was impossible to have a conversation with Flaxen. Like Papa Daan, he had become a stuttering fool in expensive designer clothes. He had separated from Brigitte and lived in the factory where his furniture was conceived and where he underpaid his employees, paid them late or didn't pay them at all.

While Tokyo was declining, Ghent was getting back on its feet thanks to Japanese capital pumped into the restoration of her old buildings, which were, once sanitised, a sought-after holiday and wedding destination for the Japanese. I did not like what they were doing to my old city with her creaking walls. She was sandblasted, her statues restored to shing golden and copper. She was genuinely old, but she looked like kitsch now. She was no longer my good old blackened, stinking Ghent, where rugged stage plays like *Red Harvest* were made. She was instead a whore with too much bling.

The *Mystic Lamb* by the van Eijk brothers in the Saint Baafs Cathedral was put in a giant glass box so that it could not be opened and closed before the viewer any longer. The man who had opened and closed the medieval triptych for the past twenty years was sitting behind a cash register in front of the glass box, the inside of the triptych showing. The point of the whole triptych was that you first looked at it while it was closed, where the colours are earthly and the figures humble. When it was opened, heaven's splendour rolled over the viewer in bold reds, yellows, greens and blues, almost as if a carcass is opened and its intestines are exposed.

In Japan, the story of filmmaker Itami uncovered the more sinister side of the economic bubble. Itami was fearless. His films satirised Japanese society. Every movie was about money, power and food. Itami's father was a prominent writer and director of satirical films. Itami began filming only at age fifty and worked many jobs during the eighties: as an actor, TV host, essayist, amateur boxer, translator of American novels, and graphic designer.

"The movies were my father's business. It was too high a mountain for me to climb," he said when I interviewed him in the hospital. "But when I turned fifty, I felt I could climb the mountain."

His father's death in 1946 from tuberculosis left a strong impression. He debuted in 1984 with *The Funeral*, about a family's dynamics during funeral preparations. It won five Japanese Academy Awards. Itami's fame continued with his ramen Western, *Tanpopo*.

The 1980s were lucrative for the yakuza. They had, since the end of WWII, operated on the fringes, hidden away in gambling parlours. When the boom hit, they wanted in on the action, played the stock market, bought real estate, and manipulated the booming building industry. They infiltrated companies and politics, bought the police, and took their gang wars to the streets.

Japanese citizens were fed up with it and organised demonstrations and lawsuits. At the time of its release, *Minbo no onna: the Gentle Art of*

Japanese Extortion was hailed as the most realistic depiction of crime and corruption in Japan. The yakuza were portrayed as sentimental rogues. The film provided the public with a manual for defeating them.

While the yakuza were raking in money, so was Itami. The success of *The Funeral* had pushed him into a much higher tax bracket, and he was hit with a very high tax bill. This inspired him to make *The Taxing Woman* (1987) and *The Return of the Taxing Woman* (1988), both of which exposed the tax collection process in Japan.

A series of financial scandals involving the yakuza was revealed when the boom went bust. Itami's observations of the economic upheaval were channelled into *Minbo no onna*, where he aimed directly at the yakuza. The movie is set inside a hotel full of yakuza. The hotel owner attempts to get rid of them. A lawyer, played by Nobuko Miyamoto, calls the bluff of the yakuza and uses legal tricks against them. The film shows what usually happens next: a citizen calls the police, the yakuza gets a slap on the wrist, and the next day they're back in business.

Historically, Japanese films had romanticised the yakuza as Robin Hood-like figures and modern-day samurai. In *Minbo no onna*, they are portrayed as idiots who make working-class people's lives miserable.

After *Minbo no onna* was released, the police patrolled Itami's home and advised him on what to do if attacked.

One week later, Itami was assaulted with knives. They sliced deep wounds into his face, neck, and arms.

"They cut very slowly. They took their time. They could have killed me if they wanted to," Itami said in his hospital bed.

"They escaped into a black car. I went into my house, dripping with blood, and told my wife to call an ambulance."

During his hospital stay, Itami wrote a letter to the public:

"Yakuza must not be allowed to deprive us of our freedom through violence and intimidation, and this is the message of my movie. What worries me most about this incident is that people might think that the yakuza really

are scary. It would be a shame if people were disheartened just when the public is beginning to stand up against organised crime."

The police arrested the men, but they would not confess to who ordered the attack.

They received prison sentences of four and five years.

After leaving the hospital, Itami returned to promoting *Minbo no onna.*

Scarred-faced, he showed reporters photographs of his wounds.

"The fact that I was attacked proves that what I pointed out in my film was real. I pointed out the truth".

Itami became a symbol of a modern Japan that no longer accepted the yakuza as a fixed part of society.

Five years later, it was rumoured that Itami's next film was about the relationship between Goto-gumi, a large yakuza gang, and Soka Gakkai, a Japanese religious organisation.

In 1997, *Flash Magazine* was preparing a story that alleged the then 64-year-old Itami was having an affair with a 26-year-old woman. It showed photos of Itami and the woman walking down the street and dining at a restaurant. The woman allegedly told the tabloid that Itami enjoyed 'unusual sex games' and had given her a large sum of money. The tabloid gave Itami a chance to tell his side of the story. Itami replied that he had interviewed the woman for a film he was making about office workers. He gave her a loan to help her move to Tokyo to shoot the film. Two days before the article's release, Itami allegedly leapt to his death from the roof of his office.

A picture of Nobuko Miyamoto was left on the computer screen, and in his note, he referred to her as "the best wife, mother and actress in Japan".

His family and friends were suspicious.

Itami satirised Japanese traditions, yet committing suicide to preserve honour was authentically Japanese. And why was the note printed from his computer and not handwritten?

WOMEN!

For his book *Tokyo Vice*, journalist Jake Adelstein interviewed yakuza members who worked for Tadamasa Goto, the founder of Goto-gumi. It was rumoured Goto was the one who put the hit out on Itami. The crime boss wrote in his autobiography,

"Minbo no onna was an unpleasant movie. It insults the yakuza, it ridicules us — but while I didn't give the order, when I found out that one of my boys had gone out and slashed him up, I was proud of him."

While researching his book, Adelstein befriended a leading anti-organised crime lawyer, Igari Toshiro, who was found dead in 2010 with his wrists slashed while writing a book about the yakuza. Adelstein asked Toshiro why he continued his risky line of work. Toshiro explained: "If you run away, you'll be chased for the rest of your life. And if you're being chased, eventually, what is chasing you will catch up. Step back, and you're dead already. You can only stand your ground and pursue. Because that's the right thing to do and the only thing to do."

Miyamoto remained under police protection for twenty years after Itami's death.

Towards the end of *Minbo no onna*, the main character recalls her father's last words before his death at the hands of the yakuza: "Everybody dies sometime, and it is better to die for your beliefs than live as a coward. Remember that always."

Ichi-go ichi-e

I embarked on the novel *Ichi-go ichi-e,* which celebrated my relationship with the city, her people and my friendships within her. One of these friends was Carrie, the American friend and colleague I often danced with all night.

In 1992, I received a letter from an old friend of Dad's, the bass player of Dad's band, Arie. I had given Arie a painting a long time ago when I had an exhibition of paintings together with Dad in a gallery in Amersfoort. Arie had returned daily to look at the painting, which has hung in its house ever since.

I had not heard from Arie since then, I must have been sixteen, but I had heard that he had spent much of his life in an institution for the mentally ill.

In the letter, Arie announced that he was coming to Japan and asked what he should bring and if I would like to meet up with him. He was playing with his jazz band at the theme park *Huis ten Bosch* in Nagasaki. The letter contained two tickets for the opening.

My research revealed that *Huis ten Bosch* was a theme park in Sasebo, Nagasaki. It recreated the Netherlands by displaying life-sized copies of old Dutch buildings. The name *Huis Ten Bosch* translates into English as "House in the Woods", the name of one residence of the Dutch Royal Family.

The theme park featured Dutch-style hotels, villas, theatres, museums, shops and restaurants, canals, windmills, amusement rides, and a park planted with tulips.

It was on Hario Island, an area of reclaimed marshland on the coast of Kyushu facing Omura. This location reflected the historical ties between the Netherlands and Japan, which began in 1609 when the Dutch opened a trading post in Hirado, off the coast of Kyushu.

Although familiar with the history, I had been unaware of the theme park until I received Arie's letter.

At work, I told Carrie about the letter from Arie and the two tickets, which cost a fortune. Carrie immediately wanted to go. I would not have gone without her enthusiasm.

We took the train from Tokyo, then a boat from Nagasaki. A Dutch city arose on the horizon. The boat moored and on the pier stood a man with white curly hair in a pillar of sunlight. He waved. Light seemed to pour out of him. It was Arie.

I fell in love with him then and there.

There was no escaping it.

Dopamine, oxytocin, adrenaline, and vasopressin began surging through me on that pier. An increased blood flow to my brain's pleasure centre released adrenaline and norepinephrine hormones into my body. I had sweaty palms, my heart skipped beats, and I experienced elation, craving, and focused attention. My mind was on one track: I had to have this man. Oxytocin created stellar feelings of sudden happiness. The reduction of serotonin in my brain caused me to be obsessed with this man. In my smitten brain, where the amygdala and frontal and prefrontal cortices demonstrated sudden diminished activity, my critical thinking abilities weren't fully functioning. It was in such a state that I experienced the opening of *Huis ten Bosch*. For the first time since its appearance, even the shadow of the Spirit of the Fox was gone.

***

END OF BOOK 1

Read further:

Women!
Book 3: Journey to the Edge

ABOUT THE BOOK

Women! is a genre-defying novel that blurs the lines between memoir and fiction as it explores the unreliability of memories. In this trilogy, Shan takes the reader on a bumpy ride through different stages of life and delves into the complex dynamics of family, love, and self-discovery.

Book 1: "Crying Mothers" is a vivid recollection of a European childhood set during The Summer of Love and how women and children thrived (or not) in that era.

Book 2: "The Spirit of the Fox" unravels the intricacies of womanhood as Shan embarks on a quest for identity and meaning with her psychiatrist, Dr Vossberg.

Book 3: "Journey to the Edge of the Earth" propels readers into an extraordinary last adventure, where Shan ventures beyond the confines of the familiar to discover untamed landscapes, both within and without.

"Women!" is a thought-provoking trilogy that challenges conventional storytelling, offering a remarkable reading experience that will linger in readers' minds long after they turn the last page.

ABOUT THE AUTHOR

Shan sees herself as "the rockstar of the European memoir", and Clear Mind Press agrees.

Shan's debut novella is *The Carpetbaggers of Mbantua*, published in 2022 by Clear Mind Press.

Her second book, Woman!, consists of three large volumes, of which *The Spirit of the Fox* is the second.

For more about Shan, go to:

https://www.clearmindpress.com/shan

www.ingramcontent.com/pod-product-compliance
Lightning Source LLC
Chambersburg PA
CBHW050314010526
44107CB00055B/2243